CYCLOPÆDIA

or, an

Universal Dictionary of ARTS and SCIENCES

(Heraldry and the Military Arts)

CYCLOPÆDIA

or, an

Universal Dictionary

of the

ARTS and SCIENCES

VOL III

Transcribed and abridged

by Anthony Charles Bravo

Bibliographical Note

This edition is an abridged republication of a work by Ephraim Chambers in two
volumes, with some additional entries from the two volume addendum by Abraham
Rees, published in 1749.

ISBN-10: 0-9814867-5-4
ISBN-13: 978-0-9814867-5-8

Published by Bravo Publishing.

EDITORS PREFACE

This book is an abridged version of the Cyclopaedia published by Ephraim Chambers (1680 – 1740), in two volumes in 1728. A few additional entries have been added from the four volume set published by Abraham Rees (1743 – 1825), in 1774, to round out some of the sparser articles. The abridgement consists primarily of those entries referring to heraldry and the military arts, thus providing an insight into the state of warcraft and armoury in the seventeenth and early eighteenth centuries. Note that most of the original spelling and punctuation has been retained.

Although we know little of Mr. Chambers life, he is credited with being the first to compile and publish an encyclopaedia. The Encyclopaedia Britannica, for example, was first published in 1771. Apparently, Mr. Chambers was inspired by John Harris' (1666 – 1719), Lexicon Technicum, published in 1704, which was considered more of a dictionary than an encyclopaedia, and decided he could improve upon the work. Abraham Rees added two more volumes, published as a supplement in one instance, and as a four-volume set re-arranged and re-written.

Mr, Chambers describes his Cyclopaedia in the preface to the work, "It may be even said, that if the System be an Improvement upon the Dictionary; the Dictionary is some Advantage to the System; and that this is perhaps the only Way wherein the whole Circle of Body of Knowledge can be deliver'd. In any other Form, many thousand Things must necessarily be hid and overlook'd : All the Pins, the Joints, the binding of the Fabrick must be invisible of course; all the lesser Parts whatsoever, must be in some measure swallowed up in the Whole. The Imagination, stretch'd and amplified to take in so large a Structure, can have but a very general, indistinguishing Perception of any of the Parts. Whereas the Parts are not less Matter of Knowledge when taken separately, than when put together. Nay, and in strictness, as our Ideas are all Singulars or Individuals, and as everything that exists is one; it seems more natural to consider Knowledge in its proper Parts, i.c. as divided into separate Articles denoted by different Terms; than to consider the whole Assemblage of it in its utmost Composition : which is a thing merely artificial and imaginary."

"And yet the latter Way must be allow'd to have many and real Advantages over the former; which in truth is only of use and significance as it partakes thereof : For this Reason, that all Writing in its own Nature is artificial; and that the Imagination is really the Faculty it immediately applies to. Hence it should follow, that the most advantageous way, is to make use of both Methods : To consider every Point both as a Part; to help the Imagination to the Whole : and as a Whole, to help it to every Part. Which is the View in the present Work – so far as the many and great Difficulties we have to labour under would allow us to pursue it."

"In this view we have endeavoured to give the Substance of what has been hitherto found in the several Branches of Knowledge both natural and artificial; that is, of Nature, *first*, as she appears to our Senses; either spontaneously, as in Natural History; or with the Assistance of Art, as in Anatomy, Chymistry, Medicine, Agriculture, &c. *Secondly*, to our Imagination; as in Grammar, Rhetorick, Poetry, &c. *Thirdly*, to our Reason;

as in Physicks, Metaphysicks, Logicks, and Mathematicks. With the several subordinate Arts arising from each; as Architecture, Painting, Sculpture, Trade, Manu-factures, Policy, Law, &c. and numerous remote Particulars, not immediately reducible to any of these Heads; as Heraldry, Philology, Antiquities, Customs, &c."

Note that entries bounded by square brackets were not in the original work and have been added here for completeness. Also note that the heraldry and fortification images are actual photos of a late edition Cyclopaedia that I owned in 2009.

A.C. Bravo, 2014

TO THE

K I N G

SIR,

The ARTS and SCIENCES humbly crave Audience of Your Majesty. The near Concern they have in the Happiness of a People, assures 'em of the favourable Attention of a Prince who makes that Happiness his own. 'Tis by These, the Parsimony of Nature is supplied, and Life render'd easy and agreeable under its numerous Infirmities. By these the Mind is reclaim'd from its native Wildness; and enrich'd with Sentiments which lead to Virtue and Glory. 'Tis these, in fine, that make the Difference between your Majesty's Subjects, and the Savages of *Canada*, or the *Cape of Good Hope*.

THE Protection of the Arts has ever been esteemed the proper Province of the Great. 'Tis a Branch of the regal Office; which a Prince, like Your Majesty, equal to the whole Charge of the Crown, will not suffer to be alienated into other Hands. From this, do the first and most distinguish'd Names in the List of Fame, derive a large Share of their Glory : and if there by any Age or Nation more conspicuous than the rest, and which is look'd on with Envy by our own; 'tis that wherein the Sovereigns have signaliz'd themselves most in this Quality. Indeed, the Time seems at hand, when we are no longer to envy Rome her AUGUSTUS and AUGUSTAN AGE, but Rome in her turn shall envy ours.

SOMETHING extraordinary is apparently intended by Providence in calling such a Prince, so such a People : A Prince who feels a generous Impulse to devote his Cares and all his Toils to the Welfare of Mankind; and a People conspiring with unexampled Ardor and Unanimity to all his glorious Views. Some of our best Princes have had their Hands ty'd down; check'd by reluctant Factions, who opposed every nobler Design : Your Majesty has found the happy Secret, to make even Contention do you Homage; and turn Opposition itself into Approbation, and Applause.

THERE is a Time reserv'd in Fate for every Nation to arrive at its Height; and the uppermost Place on the Terrestrial Ball is held successively by several States. May not the numerous Presages which usher in Your Majesty's Reign, give us room to expect that our Turn is next; and that what Greece was under *Alexander*, and *Rome* under *Augustus Caesar*, *Britain* shall be under GEORGE and CAROLINE?

BUT even this were to under-rate our Hopes, which are rais'd, by Your Majesty, to something still more truly glorious. Greatness, so fondly coveted, has already cost the World very dear; and, tho still pursued by unthinking Men under almost every Shape, is only desirable in a few. Of it self it is rather an Object of Terror and Alarm, than Delight; and at best only pleases, when joyn'd with something naturally amiable. From the Practice of your Majesty, Men may correct their Sentiments, and learn, that Greatness has no Charm except when founded in Goodness. To be Great, and a King, is but a small Matter with Your Majesty; 'tis a Quality many others enjoy in common with You, and to which some have even been doom'd, to their Infamy : 'tis what Herdo was, and Nebuchadnezzar was; and Nero and Domitian were. But, while other Princes chuse to be great in what is destructive, and others in things wholly indifferent; 'tis Your Majesty's Praise to be great in what is the Perfection of our Nature, and that whereby we approach nearest the Deity. Happy Choice! to use Power only as a Means of rendering your Beneficence more diffulsive : and thus make Power and Royalty minister to the Happiness of Mankind, which they have too often invaded.

THE Work I presume to lay at Your Majesty's Feet, is an Attempt towards a Survey of the Republick of Learning, as it stands at the Beginning of Your Majesty's auspicious Reign. We have here the Boundary that circumscribes our present Prospect; and separates the known, from the unknown Parts of the Intelligible World. Under Your Majesty's Princely Influence and Encouragement, we promise our selves this Boundary will be removed, and the Prospect extended far into the other Hemisphere. Methinks I see Trophies erecting to Your Majesty in the yet undiscover'd Regions of Science; and Your Majesty's Name inscribed to Inventions as present held impossible.

I am, with all Sincerity and Devotion,

May it please Your MAJESTY,

Your Majesty's most Dutiful,

and Obedient Subject,

and Servant,

Ephraim Chambers.

HERALDRY

𝔄

ABASED, ABAISSÉ, is applied to the vol, or wings of eagles, &c. when the tip, or angle looks downward toward the point of the shield; or when the wings are shut : the natural way of bearing them being spread, with the tip pointing to the chief, or the angles.

A chevron, a pale, bend, &c. are said to be *abased,* when their points terminate in, or below, the centre of the shield. Again, an ordinary is said to be *abased,* when below its due situation. Thus, the commanders of the order of *Malta*, who have chiefs in their own arms, are obliged to *abase* them under those of the religion.

ABATEMENT, something added to a coat-armor to diminish its proper value and dignity, and note some dishonourable action, or stain in the character of the person who bears it. It is a little controverted among authors, whether heraldry allows of any such thing as regular *Abatements. Leigh*[1] and *Guillem*[2], without any scruple to their validity, give us several kinds.

Abatements, according to the last of those writers, are either made by reversion or diminution. Reversion is either turning the whole escutcheon upside down; or the adding another escutcheon, inverted, in the former. Diminution is the blemishing any part by adding a stain, or mark of diminution : such are a delf, point dexter, a point champain, a plain point, a gore sinister, and a gusset. It may be added that these marks must always be either tawny, or murrey; otherwise, instead of diminutions, they become additions of honour.

The last editor of *Guillim* discards the whole notion of *Abatements* as a chimera. He alledges that no one instance is to be met withal of such bearing; and that it implies a contradiction to suppose it. Arms, being *insignia*

---

[1] Gerard Legh (died 1563), was an English lawyer who also wrote books on heraldry.
[2] John Guillim (c. 1565 – 1621), was an antiquarian and officer of arms at the College of Arms in London.

nobilitatis & honoris, cannot admit of a mark of infamy, without ceasing to be arms, and become badges of disgrace; which all would covet to lay aside. Add, that as no hereditary honour can be actually diminished; so neither can the marks thereof. Both, indeed, may be forfeited, as in the case of treason, where the escutcheon is totally reversed, to intimate a total suppression of the honour.

Some instances, however, are produced to the contrary by *Columbiere*[1] and others. But these, though they show some extraordinary resentments of princes for offences committed in their presence, do not amount to a proof of such custom or practice; much less authorize the being of particular badges in the hands of inferior officers, as kings at arms.

ACCOLADE, a ceremony anciently used in the conferring of knighthood. The *Accolade* consisted in the king's laying his arms about the young knight's neck, and embracing him in token of friendship. After the *Accolade* the prince giving him a little blow on the shoulder with the flat of a sword, he forthwith entered into the profession of arms. The word is *French* and literally denotes an embrace or hugging; being formed of *ad*, to; and *col* or *collum*, neck.

AIGLETTE. See the article *Eaglet*.

AIGUISCÉ, AIGUISSÉ, or **EGUISCÉ**, a term applied to a cross when its four ends are sharpened, so however as to terminate in obtuse angles. The cross *aiguiscé* differs from the cross fitchee, in that the latter goes tapering by degrees to a sharp point; whereas only the ends of the former are tapered. See *Fitchee*.

ALAISEE, the same with *Humetty*.

ARGENT, signifies the colour white, used in the coats of gentlemen, knights, and baronets. Barons and all nobles have the white colour called *pearl*; and sovereign princes have theirs called *luna*. Without either *argent* or *or*, the heralds say there can be no good armory.

Argent is expressed in engraving by the parts being left plain, without any strokes from the graver. The word is *French*, derived from the Latin *argentum*; this colour being supposed the representation of that metal : whence the Spaniards call this field *compo de plata*, silver field.

In the doubling of mantles, where the white is supposed to represent a fur, not a metal, it may be blazoned white.

---

[1] Marcus Vulson de la Colombière (c. 1590 - 1658), or Sieur de la Colombière, was a French heraldist, historian, poet.

ARMORY is used for a branch of heraldry; being the knowledge of coat-armors, as to their blazons, and various intendments. See *Heraldry*.

ARMS, ARMORIES, is also used in heraldry, for marks of dignity and honour, regularly composed of certain figures and colours, given or authorized by sovereigns, and bore in banners, shields, coats, &c. for the distinction of persons, families, and states, and passing by descent to posterity.

They are called arms, in regard they are bore principally on the buckler, cuirasse, banners, and other apparatus of war. They are also called coats of arms, coat-armor, &c. because anciently embroidered on fur coats, &c.

Some will have the name to have been first occasioned by the ancient knights, who in their jousts and tournaments bore certain marks (which were frequently their mistress's favours) in their armor, *i.e.* their helms or shield; to distinguish them from each other.

Three flowers *de lys*, in a field azure, are the *arms* of *France*. The *arms* of *England* are three lions. In the arms of *Great Britain* are quartered the *arms* of *France, England, Scotland* and *Ireland*.

There has been a great dispute among the learned about the origin of *arms*. *Favyn*[1] will have them to have been from the beginning of the world; *Segoin*[2] from the time of *Noah*; others, from that of *Osiris*, which is supported by some passages in *Diodorus Siculus*; others from the times of the *Hebrews*, in regards *arms* were given to *Moses, Joshua*, the twelve tribes, *David*, &c. Others will have them to have taken their rise during the heroical age, and under the empires of the *Assyrians, Medes*, and *Persians*; building upon *Philostratus, Xenophon*, and *Quintus Curtius*.

Some pretend that the use of arms and the rules of blazon were regulated by *Alexander*. Others will have them to have had their original under the empire of *Augustus*; others during the inundations of the *Goths*; and others under the empire of *Charlemagne*.

Chorier[3] observes, that among the ancient *Gauls*, that each man bore a mark on his buckler, by the sight whereof he might be known to his fellows; and hence he refers the original of the *arms* of noble families. *Camden*[4] has observed something like this of the ancient *Picts*, and *Britons*, who going naked to the wars, painted their bodies with blazons, and figures of divers colours, which he supposes to have been different in different families, as they fought divided by kindreds. Yet *Spelman*[5] says, the *Saxons, Danes*, and *Normans*, first brought arms from the north into *England*; and thence into *France*.

---

[1] André Favyn (1612 - 1620), who wrote a compendious history of heraldry and other works.
[2] Charles Segoing (17th c.), was a French heraldist and royal historian.
[3] Nicolas Chorier (1612 –1692), was a French lawyer, writer, and historian.
[4] William Camden (1551 – 1623), was an English antiquarian, historian, and officer of arms.
[5] Sir *Henry Spelman* (1562-1641), was a British antiquarian.

Upon the whole it is certain, that from time immemorial, there have been symbolical marks in use among men to distinguish then in armies, and to serve as ornaments of shields and ensigns; but these marks were used arbitrarily as devices, emblems, hieroglyphics, &c. and were not regular *armories*, like ours, which are hereditary marks of the nobility of a house, regulated according to the rules of heraldry, and authorized by princes.

Before *Marius*[1], even the eagle was not the constant ensign of the *Roman* army; but they bore in their standards a wolf, leopard, or eagle indifferently, according to the fancy of the generals.

The same diversity has been observed with regard to the *French* and *English*; on which account authors are divided when they speak of the ancient *arms* of those countries. In effect, it appears from all the best authors, that the armories of houses, as well as the double names of families, were not known before the year 1000. And several have endeavoured to prove that the use of *arms* did not begin till the time of the first croisade by the Christians in the east. The truth is, it appears to have been the ancient tournaments that occasioned the fixing of armories.

Henry the Fowler[2], who regulated the tournament in *Germany*, was the first to introduce these marks of honour, which appear to be of an older standing in *Germany* than any other part of *Europe*. It was then that coats of *arms* were first instituted; which were a kind of livery composed of several bars, fillets, and colours; whence came the fess, bend, pale, chevron, and lozenge; which were some of the first elements of armories. Those who had never been concerned in any tournament had no *arms* even though they were gentlemen. Such of the nobility and gentry that crossed the sea, in the expeditions to the Holy Land, also assumed these tokens of honour to distinguish themselves.

Before these times, we find nothing on ancient tombs but crosses, with Gothic inscriptions and representations of the persons deceased. The tomb of Pope *Clement* IV, who died in 1268, is the first whereon we find any arms; nor do they appear on any coins struck before 1336. We meet with figures, it is true, much more ancient, both in standards and on medals; but nether cities nor princes had *arms* in form; nor does any author make mention of blazoning before that time.

Originally, none but nobility had the right to of bearing arms, but King *Charles* V, having ennobled the *Parisians*, by his charter in 1371, he permitted them to bear *arms*; from whose example the more eminent citizens of other places did the like.

Camden refers the original of hereditary arms in *England* to the time of the first *Norman* kings. He says their use was not established till the reign of King *Henry* III, and instances in several of the most considerable families in *England*, wherein, till that time, the son always bore different *arms* from the

---

[1] Gaius Marius (157 BC – 86 BC), was a Roman general and statesman.
[2] Henry the Fowler (876 – 936), was the Duke of Saxony from 912 and the King of Germany from 919 until his death.

father. About the same time it became the custom here in *England* for private gentlemen to bear arms; borrowing them from the lords of whom they held in see, or to whom they were most devoted.

ARMS, at present, follow the nature of titles, which being made hereditary, these are also become so; being the several marks for distinguishing of families and kindreds, as names are of persons and individuals. *Arms* make the object of the art of heraldry.

ARMS, are variously distinguished by the heralds:

Canting **ARMS**, are those wherein the figures bear an allusion to the name of the family. Such as those of the family *la Tour* in *Auvergne*, who bear a tower; that of the family of *Prado* in *Spain*, whose field is a meadow. Most authors hold these the most noble and regular, as is shown by an infinity of instances produced by Father *Varenne*[1] and *Menestrier*[2]. They are much debased when they come to make use of the rebus. See *Rebus*.

Charged **ARMS**, are such as retain their ancient integrity and value, with the addition of some new honourable charge or bearing, in consideration of some noble action.

Full or entire **ARMS**, are such as retain their primitive purity, integrity, or value; without any alterations, diminutions, abatements, or the like.
It is a rule, that the simpler and less diversified the *arms*, the more noble and ancient they are. For this reason, *Garcias Ximenes*, first king of *Navarre*, and his successors for several ages, bore only gules, without any figure at all.
The *arms* of princes of the blood, of all younger sons and junior families, are not pure and full; but distinguished and diminished by proper differences, &c. See *Differences*.

ARMS, are also said to be *parted*, *couped*, *quartered*, &c. *Arms* are said to be false and irregular when there is something in them contrary to the rules of heraldry. As, when metal is put on metal, or colour on colour, &c. The laws, and other affairs of arms, with the cognizance of offences committed therein, belong, among us, to the earl-marshal and college of *arms*.

ARRONDIE, *Cross-Arrondie*, or *rounded*, is that whose arms are composed of sections of a circle, not opposite to each other, so as to make the arm bulge out thicker in one part than another; but both the sections of each arm lie the

---

[1] Probably Bernard de Varenne, a French historian living in the late 17c and early 18th centuries.
[2] Claude-François Ménestrier (1631 –1705), was a French heraldist, a Jesuit, and attendant at the royal court.

same way, so the arm is every where of an equal thickness; and all of them terminating at the edges of the escutcheon, like the plain cross.

ASSUMPTIVE *arms*, are such as a man has right to assume of himself, in virtue of some gallant action. As, if a man who is no gentleman of blood, nor coat armor, takes a gentleman, lord, or prince, prisoner in any lawful war; he become entitled to bear the shield of such prisoner; and enjoy it to him and his heirs. The foundation hereof is that principle in military law, that the dominion of things take in lawful war passes to the conqueror.

ATCHIEVEMENT, the coat of arms of any person or family, duly marshaled with its external ornaments and supports, helmet, wreath, crest, and motto. Such are those usually hung out on the fronts of houses after the death of some considerable person, now corruptly called *hatch-ments*. The word is formed of the *French achevement*, finishing, consummation, perfection.

𝕭

BALLS, or **BALLETS**, make a frequent bearing in coat of arms, though never so called; but having according to their several colours several names, as *besants* when the colour is *or*; *plates* when *argent*; *hurts* when *azure*; *torteaux* when *gules*; *pomeis* when *vert*; *pellets* or *agresses* when *sable*; *golpes* when *purple*; *orenges* when *tanne*; and *guzes* when *sanguine*.

BAR, **BARR**, **BARRE**, denotes an ordinary nearly resembling the *fess*; from which it only differs by its narrowness, and by this, that the *bar* may be placed in part of the field, whereas the *fess* is confined to a single place. See *Fesse*.

BARRULET, is half of the closet, or the quarter of the bar.

BARRY. When an escutcheon is divided bar-ways into an even number of partitions, and consist of two or more tinctures interchangeably disposed, it is expressed in blazon by the word *barry*, and the number of pieces is to be specified. *e.gr. Barry* of so many pieces. If the divisions be odd, the field must be first named, and the number of bars expressed.

BARRY-BENDY, is when an escutcheon is divided evenly both bar and bend-ways, by lines drawn transverse and diagonal, interchangeably varying the tinctures of which it consists. Thus, he bears *barry-bendy*, *or* and *sable*. See *Tab. Herald. fig.* 4.

BARRY-PILY, is when a coat is divided as represented in *Tab. Herald. fig.* 5. Which is blazoned *barry-pily* of eight pieces.

BASTON, or **BATOON**, a kind of bend which has only one third of the usual breadth. The *baston* does not go from side to side of the escutcheon as the bend or scarf does, but is broken off short, in form of a truncheon : its use is as a mark of bastardy.

BEND, an ordinary, or bearing, formed by two lines, drawn diagonally, or a-thwart, from the upper part of the shield on the right, to the lower part on the left; being supposed to represent a shoulder-belt, or scarf worn over the shoulder. The *bend* is one of the ten honourable ordinaries, containing a third part of the field when charged, and a fifth when plain. It is sometimes indented, ingrailed, &c.

Heralds speak of a *bend dexter* and a *bend sinister*. A *bend* is subdivided into a *benlet*, or a *bandelet*, which is the sixth part of the shield; a *garter* which is the moiety of a *bend*; a *cost* which is the fourth part of a *bend*; and a *ribband* which is a moiety of a *cost*.

BEND *dexter*, is that properly and absolutely called a *bend*. The word *dexter* is usually annexed to prevent mistakes.

BEND *sinister*, which is the same what is otherwise called after the *French* heralds, a *bar*, *barre*. The *bend sinister* is subdivided into the *scarf*, or *scarp*, and the *battoon*; which latter is the fourth part of the *bend*, and the most usual mark of illegitimacy; but then it never extends itself quite a-thwart the shield, but is cut off a little at each end. When two straight lines drawn within the *bend* run nearly parallel to the outward edges of it, this is called *voiding*; and he that bears it, is said *to bear a bend voided*.

BENDY, BENDÉ, in blazonry denotes an escutcheon's being divided bend-wise into an even number of partitions. If they be odd, the field must first be named, and then the number of bends.

BILLET, a bearing in form of a long square. See *Tab. Herald. fig. 9. Billets* are said to be couched or inverted when their longest side is parallel to the top of the shield, and the shortest perpendicular. They are supposed to represent pieces of cloth of gold or silver, longer than broad, placed at a distance by way of ornament, on clothes, and afterwards translated to their coat-armour : though *Guillim* takes the billet to represent a letter sealed up. A coat is said to be *billited*, when charged with *billets*. This he bears *argent-billette*, a cross ingrailed gules by the name of *Heath*. *Bloom* says, the number of *billets* must be expressed when they are not above ten.

BLAZON, or **BLAZONRY**, the art of deciphering the arms of noble houses; or of naming all the parts in their proper and particular terms. There is this difference between *arms* and *blazon*; that the first are the devise or figures bore on the coat or shield; and *blazon* the description thereof in words.

The rules of *blazon* are: 1. To name the metal or colour of the field first : as *or*, *argent*, or *gules*, &c. 2. To name the manner of the division of the escutcheon by line, whether downright or bend-wise, and also the difference of the line, whether it be indented, ingrailed, &c. in the next place. 3. Then to name the charge that is on the field. 4. Having thus expressed the field, the division, and the charge, if there be more parts of the field occupied by the charge than one, you are to name the principal part of the field first. 5. If there by more than one kind of charge in a field, that in the chief part is to be named first. 6. To use no iteration or repetition of words in blazoning a coat, especially any of these four words, of, or, and, with. 7. The three forms of *blazon* are by metals or colours, by precious stones, and the celestial planets :

the first for private gentlemen; the second for persons ennobled with titles, such as dukes, earls, &c. and the third for emperors, kings, and princes. Though this variety of form is rejected by the *French*, from whom we had our heraldry, and by all other nations, who use but metals and colours for all degrees. 8. That metal upon metal, and colour upon colour, is false heraldry : which admits of no exception, except in the arms of *Jerusalem*, which are argent, a cross potent between four croslets, or.

Add, that when lions stand upright in a coat, they are called *rampant*; when walking forward, *passant*; when they look you in the face, *passant guardant* : in other postures they have other terms, *salient, regardant*, &c. Wolves and bears are termed after the manner of lions; griffons (instead of rampant and salient) are termed *sergeant*; lions, griffins, and eagles are also said to be *languid* and *armed*; swans, *membred*; hawks, *jessed* and *belled*; cocks, *armed, dressed, jowloped*: that is, when the tongues, claws, and bills of such creatures are found of different colours from the body. When an animal proceeds from the bottom of the ordinary, it is termed *issuant*; when over some ordinary, *jessant*; if it proceed from the middle of any ordinary, or common charge, *naissant*.

Various etymologies are given for the word *blazon* : the most probable is that which brings it from the *German, blaesen*, to blow a horn; it being the custom of those who presented themselves at the lists in the ancient tournaments, to blow a horn to notify their comings. After this the heralds sounded their trumpets, and then blazoned the arms of those who presented themselves; describing them aloud, and sometimes expatiating on the praises and high exploits of the persons who bore them.

BORDURE, or **BORDER**, a kind of addition on the limb of a shield, in the form of a hem or girdle, encompassing all round, and serving as a difference. The bordure must be about one sixth part of the breadth of the shield. *Simple bordure* is that which is the same colour or metal throughout; and is the first addition of younger brothers. There are others, *componed, countred, ingrailed, indented*, and *charged* with other pieces; which make different additions for younger brothers in several degrees.

If the line which constitutes the *bordure* be straight, and the border plain, as they call it in blazoning, the colour of the *bordure* alone is named, as, he beareth gules, a *bordure or*. If a bordure be charge with any plants or flowers, they say, *verdure* of trefoils. If it consist of ermins, vairy, or any of the furs, the term is *perflew* of ermins : if the *bordure* be charged with martlets, the word is *charged* with an enaluron of martlets, &c.

BOTTONY, or **BOTTONÉ**, is used in speaking of a cross, which terminates at each end in three knots or buttons, resembling, in some measure, three-leaved grass. A *cross bottony*, is the same with what *Segoin* terms, *croix* *trefflée*; and *Baron, globosa crux* : *Gibbon[1]*, the better to explain the form, renders it *Crux ad singulas ejus extremitates in tres gemmes vel nodos, pro trifolii specie, terminate*. He bears a cross *bottony* sable by the name of *Winwood*.

BRACED, is used in speaking of chevronels which are intermingled. He bears azure a chief or, and three chevronels *braced*, in the base of the escutcheon, by the name of *Fitz-hugh*.

---

[1] John Gibbon (1629–1718), who was a writer on heraldry.

C

CARBUNCLE, a charge or bearing consisting of eight radii or spokes; four whereof make a common cross, and the four a saltier. See *Tab. Herald. fig.* 13. Some call these radii, *battons* or *staves*; because round and enriched with buttons, or pearled like pilgrims staves; and frequently tipped or terminated with flowers-de-luces. Others blazon them royal scepters, placed in saltier, pale and fesse.

CERCELE, a *Cross cercele* is a cross, which opening at the ends, turns round both ways, like a ram's horn.

CHAPPE, the partition of an escutcheon, by lines drawn from the center of the upper edge to the three angles below : as represented in *Tab. Herald. fig.* 14. which they blazon *chappe* or, and vert.

CHARGE, is applied to any figure, or thing, bore, in an escutcheon, or coat of arms; whether it be animal, vegetable, or other matter. Too many charges are not deemed so honourable as fewer.

Charges peculiar to the art and usage of armory, as the cross, chief, pale, fesse, &c. are called *proper charges*; and frequently *ordinaries*. *Bloom* restrains the term *charges* to those additions, or rewards of honours frequently placed on escutcheons; as cantons, quarters, girons, flasques, &c.

CHECKY, is where the shield, or a part thereof, as the bordure, &c. is chequered, or divided into chequers, or squares. *See Tab Herald. fig.* 15. Where there is but one row of squares it is not properly called *checky*, but *countercomponed*.

Checky according to *Colombierre*, is one of the most noble and ancient figures in all armory; and ought never to be given but to persons who have distinguished themselves in war : for it represents a chess-board, which it self is a representation of a field of battle. The pawns and men, placed on both sides, represent the soldiers of the two armies; which move, advance, or retire, according to the will of the two gamesters, who are the generals.

Checky is always composed of metal and colour. Some authors would have it ranked among the sorts of furs. When the whole escutcheon is chequered, it should ordinarily contain six ranges : there is no need of blazoning to express them; only it must be observed, to begin to blazon by the first square in chief on the dexter side. So that if that be *or*, and next *gules*, the house or family is said to bear *check*, *or* and *gules*. When the whole shield is not chequered, but only the chief, a bend, cross, or the like, the number of ranges should be expressed.

CHEVALIER, a *French* term, ordinarily signifying a knight. It is used in heraldry to signify any *Cavalier*, or horseman, armed at all points; by the *Romans cataphractus eques*, now out of use, and only to be seen in coat-armour. The word is formed of the *French cheval*, from that of the *Latin cavallus*.

CHEVELLE, a term used by the *French* heralds, to express a head where the hair is a different colour from the rest of the head.

CHEVRON, or **CHEVERON**, one of the honourable ordinaries of a shield; representing two rafters of a house joined together, without any division. If descends from the chief to the extremities of the coat, in the form of a pair of compasses half open. Thus, he bears, gules, as *Chevron* argent. See *Tab. Herald. fig.* 16.

The *Chevron* is the symbol of protection, say some, or of constancy according to others; some say it represents the knights spurs; other the head attire of priestesses; others a piece of the list, or the fence or barrier of a park.

When it is alone, it should take up the third part of the coat; when it is accompanied by other bearings, its breadth must be adjusted thereby. It is bore divers ways; sometimes in chief, sometimes in base, sometimes enarched, sometimes reversed, &c. The *Chevron* is sometimes charge with another *chevron* of its own height.

Two *Chevrons* are allowed in the same field, but not more; when they exceed that number, they are called *chevronwise*, or *chevronels*. There are *Chevrons* of several pieces.

A *Chevron* is said to be *abased* when its point does not approach the head of the chief, nor reach further than the middle of the coat; *mutilated* when it does not touch the extremes of the coat; *cloven* when the upper point is taken off, so that the pieces only touch at one of the angles; *couched* when on point is turned towards one side of the escutcheon; *divided* when the branches are of several metals, or when the metal is opposed to colour; *inverted* when the point is towards the point of the coat, and its branches towards the chief.

A coat is said to be *chevroned* when filled with an equal number of *chevrons* of colour and metal. *Counterchevroned* is when it is so divided, as that colour is opposed to metal, and vice versa.

Per **CHEVRON**, *or party per* **CHEVRON**, is when the field is divided by only two single lines, rising from the two base points, and meeting in a point above, as the *chevron* does.

CHEVRONEL, a diminutive of *chevron*, and as such only contains half a *chevron*.

CHEVRONNE, or **CHEVRONY**, signifies the parting of a shield, several times *Chevronwise*. *Gibbon* says, *Chevronne* of six.

CHIEF, is the upper part of the escutcheon, reaching quite across from side to side. The arms of *France* are three golden flowers de lys, in a field azure; two in *chief*, and one in point.

CHIEF is more particularly used for one of the honourable ordinaries, placed athwart the top of the coat, and containing one third part of its height. When the escutcheon is cut in stone, or *in relievo*, the chief stands out prominent beyond the rest; and is supposed to represent the diadem of the ancient kings and prelates; or the cask of the knights.

It is frequently without any ornament; sometimes it is charged with other bearings; sometimes is of a different colour or metal from the rest of the coat.

The line that bounds it at bottom is sometimes straight, sometimes indented, engrailed, embattled, lozenge, &c. Thus, say they, The field is gules, the *chief* argent, &c. again, he bears gules, a *chief* crenele, or embatteled argent.

Sometimes one *chief* is born on another, expressed by a line drawn along the upper part of the *chief*: when the line is along the under part, it is called a *Fillet*. The first is an addition of honour, the second of diminution.

The *chief* is said to be *abased* when it is detached from the upper edge of the coat, by the colour of the field which is over it; and which retrenches from it one third of its height. We also say, a *chief* is *chevroned*, *paled*, or *bended*, when it has a chevron, pale, or bend contiguous to it, and of the same colour as itself. A *chief* is said to be supported, when the two thirds at top are of the colour as the field, and at bottom of a different colour.

CLARION, is a bearing represented in *Tab. Herald. fig.* 36. He bears ruby, three *Clarions* topaz, being the arms of the earl of *Bath*, by the name of *Granville*. *Guillim* takes these *Clarions* to be a kind of old-fashioned trumpet; but others think they represent the rudders of a ship; others a rest for a lance.

COMBATANT, is the heralds word for two beasts, as lions, or boars, bore in a coat of arms in a fighting posture, erect on their hinder feet and affrontee, or their faces towards each other.

CONTRE-BEND. A bar is called *contre-bend*, or *counter-band*, because it cuts the shield contrary, and opposite ways.

They also say, *contre-chevron*, *contre-pale*, &c. when there are two ordinaries of the same nature opposite each other; so as colour opposed to metal, and metal to colour. And the coat is said to be *contre*, or *counter-paled*, *counter-bended*, *counter-fessed*, *counter-composed*, *counter-barred* when so divided.

Counter-quartered is when of the quarters is quartered again : hence also *counter-flowered*, *counter-coloured*, &c. Animals are said to be *counter-passant*, when one passes on one side, and another on another.

CORDED. A *cross corded*, some authors take for a cross wound or wrenched about with *cords*; though others, with more probability, take it for a cross made of two pieces of *cord*.

COTICE, or **COTISE**, the fourth part of the bend; which, with us, is seldom ever born but in couples, with a bend between them : whence, probably, the name; from the *French coté*, side; they being born, as it were, aside of the bend. A bend thus bordered is said to be *cotised, cotice*. He bears sable on a bend *cotised* argent three cinque-foils. See *Tab. Herald. fig.* 61.

COUCHANT, is understood of a lion or other beast, when lying down; but with his head lifted up : which distinguishes the posture of *couchant* from *dormant*, wherein he is supposed quite stretched out and asleep.

COUCHÉ, denotes any thing laid down all along; thus a *chevron couché* is a *chevron* lying sideways with the two ends on one side of the shield, which should properly rest on the base.

COUNTER-BARRY, or **CONTRE-BARRÉ**, is used by the *French* heralds for what we more ordinarily call *bendy sinister per bend counterchanged*.

COUNTER-BENDY, or **CONTRE-BENDÉ**, is used by the *French* to express what we ordinarily call *bendy of six per bend sinister counter-charged*.

COUNTER-CHANGED, is when there is a mutual changing of the colours of the field and charge in an escutcheon, by means of one or more lines of partition. Thus, in the coat of the famous *Chaucer*, he beareth *party per pale argent and gules, a bend countercharged*; that is that part of the bend, which is in that side of the escutcheon which is argent, is gules; and that part of which is on the other is argent. *Tab. Herald. fig.* 50.

COUNTER-CHEVRONED, denotes a shield *chevrony*, or parted by some line of partition.

COUNTER-COMPONED, or **CONTRE-COMPONÉ**, or **COUNTER-COMPONY**, is when a bordure is compounded of two ranks of panes; as represented in *Tab. Herald. fig.* 51. When it consist of but one rank it is called *componed*; and when of more than two, *checky*.

COUNTER-PALED, CONTRE-PALÉ, is when the escutcheon is divided into twelve pales parted per fesse, the two colours being counter-changed : so that the upper are of one colour or metal, and the lower of another.

COUNTER-PASSANT, is when two lions are in a coat of arms, and one appears to be passing or walking quite the contrary way from the other.

COUNTER-POINTED, by the *French* called *contre-pointé*, is when two chevrons in one escutcheon meet in the points; the one rising as usual from the base, and the other inverted, falling from the chief : so that they are counter, or opposite to one another in the points. They may also be *counter-pointed* the other way; that is, when they are founded on the sides of the shield and the points meet that way; called *counter-pointed in fesse*.

COUNTER-POTENT, or *potent counter-potent*, by the *French* heralds called *contre-potence*, is reckoned a fur, as well as vair and ermine; but composed of such pieces as represent the tops of crutches, called in *French potences*, and in old *English potents*.

COUNTER-QUARTERED, called by the *French contre-escartele*, denotes the escutcheon, after being quartered, to have each quarter again divided into two : so that there are eight quarters or divisions.

COUNTER-SALIENT, is when two beasts are borne in a coat of arms in a posture of leaping from one another directly the contrary way.

COUNTER-TRIPPING, is when two beasts are born in a coat of arms tripping, *i.e.* in a walking posture, and the head of the one to the tail of the other.

COUPED, COUPÉ, expresses a head, limb, or other thing, in an escutcheon which is borne as if cut clear and even off from the trunk; in opposition to its being forcibly torn off, which they call *erased*. Thus, the arms of *Ulster*, is a dexter hand *couped*, or cut off at the wrist.

COUPED, COUPEÉ, is also used to denote such crosses, bar, bends, chevrons, &c. as do not touch the sides of the escutcheon, but are, as it were, cut off from them.

COUPLE *close*, the fourth part of a chevron; never borne but in pairs, except a chevron be between, sayeth *Guillim*; though *Bloom* gives an instance to the contrary.

COUSU, is used in the same sense as *remply*, *viz.* for piece of another colour or metal, placed on an ordinary as if it was sewed on; which the word in the

French language naturally implies. By reason the additional piece is not properly on the field, but in the nature of a thing sewed on, *adsutus*. This is generally of colour on colour, or metal on metal, contrary to the general rule of heraldry.

COUVERT, denotes something like a piece of hanging, or a pavilion falling over the top of a chief, or other ordinary; so as not to hide, but only be a covering thereto.

CRAMPONEÉ. A *cross cramponeé*, is that which at each end has a *cramp*, or square piece coming from it. As represented in *Tab. Herald. fig.* 52.

CRENELLÉ, *imbattled*, is when any honourable ordinary is dented, after the manner of battlements of a wall. The *French* word comes from *cren*, a notch, or interval; the *English* from its being a place of fighting, or battle. *Upton[1]*, in *Latin*, calls this *imbatullatum*, a word forged from the *English*; but most others term it *pinnatum*, from *pinna*, a battlement. The origin hereof is, doubtless, from the figures of such walls being given to warriors, either for having been the first at mounting, or the chief in defending them.

CRESCENT, is a bearing in form of a half moon. The *crescent* is frequently used as a difference in coat-armor, to distinguish it for that of a second brother, or junior family.

The figure of the *crescent* is the *Turkish* symbol; or rather, it is that of the city of *Byzantium*, which bore this device from all antiquity; as appears from medals struck in honour of *Augustus*, *Trajan*, &c. The *Ottomans* bear sinople, a *crescent* montant, argent.

The crescent is sometimes *montant*, *i.e.* its points look towards the top of the chief, which its most ordinary representation : whence some contend, that the *crescent*, absolutely so called, implies that situation; though others blazon it *montant*, when the horns are towards the dexter side of the escutcheon, when others call it *incroissant*.

Crescents are said to be *adossed*, when their backs or thickest parts are turned towards each other; their points looking to the sides of the shield.

Crescent inverted, is that whose points look towards the bottom : turned *crescents* are those placed like those *adossed*; the difference is that all their points look to the dexter side of the shield : *con-turned crescents*, on the contrary, look to the sinister side : affronted or *appointed crescents*, are contrary to the *adossed*, the points looking towards each other.

CREST, denotes the uppermost part of an armoury; or that rising over the cask or helmet. Next to the mantle, says *Guillim*, the *crest* or *cognizance*

---

[1] Nicholas Upton (died 1457), was an English scholar and cleric, preceptor of Salisbury, and writer on heraldry and the art of war.

claims the highest place; being seated on the most eminent part of the helmet; yet so as to admit an interposition of some escrol, wreath, chapeau, crown, &c. The *crest* of the arms of *England* is a lion passant gardant, crowned with an imperial crown; that of *France* a flower-de-lys.

In the ancient tournaments, the cavaliers had plumes of feathers, especially of ostriches and herons, for their *crests*; these tufts they called *plumarts*; and were placed in tubes, on the tops of high caps or bonnets. Some had their *crests* of leather; others of parchment, pastboard, &c. painted or varnished to keep out the weather; other of steel, wood, &c. on which were sometimes represented a member or ordinary of the coat; as an eagle, flower-de-lys, &c. but never any of those called honourable ordinaries, as pale, fesse, &c. The *crests* were changeable at pleasure; being reputed no other than as an arbitrary devise or ornament.

Herodotus attributes the rise of crests to the *Carions*, who first bore features on their casks, and painted figures on their bucklers; whence the *Persians* called them cocks.

The oldest of the heathen gods are said to have wore *crests*, even before arms were made of iron and steel. *Jupiter Ammon* bore a ram's head for a *crest*; *Mars* that of a lion, or a tyger casting out fire at his mouth or nostrils. *Alexander* the great wore for a crest a ram's head, to inculcate that he was the son of *Jupiter Ammon*; *Julius Caesar* sometimes bore a star, to denote that he was descended from *Venus*; and sometimes the head of a bull, or an elephant with his trunk; and sometimes the wolf that suckled *Romulus* and *Remus*.

The Christians, in their first religious wars, were wont to wear a cross darting forth rays for their *crests*, as well as on their shields and banners.

The ancient warriors wore *crests* to strike terror in the enemies, at the sight of spoils of animals they had killed; or to give them the more formidable mien, by making them appear taller, &c. *Plutarch* observes, that the *crest* of *Pyrrhus* was a bunch of feathers, with a stag's horns; and *Diodorus Siculus*, that the kings of *Egypt*, lion's heads, bulls, or dragons.

The *crest* is esteemed a greater mark of nobility than the armoury, as being bore at tournaments; to which none were admitted till they had given proof of their nobility. Sometimes it serves to distinguish the several branches of a family. It has served on occasion as the distinguishing badge of factions.

Sometimes the *crest* is taken from the device; but more usually it is formed of some piece of the arms : thus the emperor's *crest* is an eagle; that of *Castille*, a castle, &c. Families that exchange arms, as have done the houses of *Brunswic* and *Cologne*, do not change their *crests*; the first still retain the horse, the latter the mermaid.

CROISSANTÉ. *Croix criossanté* is a cross crescented; that is, having a crescent, or half-moon, fixed on each end thereof.

CROSS, is defined by *Guillim*, an ordinary composed of four-fold lines, whereof two are perpendicular, and the other two transverse; for so we must conceive if then, though they be not drawn throughout, but meet by couples, in four right angles, near the fesse point of the escutcheon.

The content of a *cross* is not always the same : for when it is not charged, nor accompanied, it has only the fifth part of the field; but if it be charged, it must contain a third part thereof.

This bearing was first bestowed on such as had performed, or at least undertaken, some service for Christ, and the Christian profession; and is held, by divers, the most honourable charge in all heraldry. What brought it into such frequent use, was the ancient expeditions into the holy land; and the holy war pilgrims, after their pilgrimage, taking the cross for their cognizance; and the ensign of that war being the *cross*.

In those wars, says *Mackenzy[1]*, the *Scotts* carried St. *Andrew's* cross. The *French* a *cross* argent; the *English* a *cross* or; the *Germans* sable; the *Italians* azure; the *Spaniards* gules.

St. *George's* cross, or the *red cross*, in a field argent, is now the standard of *England*; that saint being the reputed patron of this nation.

Guillim enumerates thirty-nine different sorts of crosses used in heraldry. *Colombiere* makes seventy-two distinct sorts of crosses. These are the various crosses we find in the aforesaid authors; which some may think too many, as not being at all used in England : but heraldry extends to all countries, and all terms used require to be explained.

Nor is it only in *crosses* that the variety is so great; the like is found in many other bearings, and particularly in lions, and the parts of them; whereof the same *Colombiere* gives us no less than ninety-six varieties. *Leigh[2]* mentions but forty-six several *crosses*; *Sylvanus Morgan[3]*, twenty six; *Upton* thirty; *Johannes de Bado Aureo*, twelve; and so others whom it is needless to mention.

Upton owns he dares not presume to ascertain all the various crosses used in arms, for that they are at present almost innumerable : and therefore he only takes notice of such as he had seen in his own time.

CROSSELET, *little cro*ss, a diminutive of *cross*, used in heraldry, where we frequently see the shield covered in *crosselets*; also fesses, or other honourable ordinaries charged or accompanied with *crosselets*. Crosses themselves frequently terminate in *crosselets*; as in *Tab. Herald. fig.* 54.

CROWN, or **CORONET**, is used for the representation of that ornament, in the mantling of an armoury; to express the dignity of the person who bears it. The *crown* here is of more antiquity even than the helmet; and was used as a symbol of victory and triumph.

---

[1] Sir George Mackenzie of Rosehaugh (ca. 1636 – 1691), was a Scottish lawyer, Lord Advocate, and author.
[2] Gerard Legh (died 1563), was an English lawyer, known as a writer on heraldry.
[3] Sylvanus Morgan (1620–1693), was an English arms-painter and author.

Radiated, or *pointed* **CROWNS**, are those of the ancient emperors; representing as some will have it, the twelve months of the year.

Pearled, or *flowered* **CROWNS**, those with pearls, or flowers of smallage, parsley, &c. Such were anciently almost all crowns, even those of sovereign princes; though they were not used in their armouries till about 200 years ago.

𝕯

DANCETTÉ, is when the outline of any bordure, or ordinary, is indented very largely; the largeness of the indentures being the only thing that distinguishes it from indented. There is also a bearing of a bend called *double Dancetté*; thus, he beareth azure, a bend *double Dancetté* argent.

DANCHE, or **DENCHÉ**, the same with indented; or, as others will have it, with *Dancetté*.

DANTELLÉ, the same with *Danché*, or rather with *Dancetté*; *viz.* a large, open indenture.

DEBRUIZED, or **DEBRUISED**, is when we would imitate the grievous restraint of any animal, which is debarred in its natural freedom, by any of the ordinaries laying over it. Thus, when a pale, &c. is born upon a beast in an escutcheon, the beast is said to be *debruized* of the pale.

DECREMENT, or **DECRESSANT**, denotes the wane, or decrease of the moon, when she is receding from the full towards the new. In this state in blazon she is called a moon-*decressant*, or *en decours*; since to call it a crescent would be improper as that term denotes an increase. The moon looking to the left side of the escutcheon is always supposed to be *decressant*: when she faces the right, she is crescent, or in her growth.

DEGRADED. A cross degraded, is a cross marked, or divided into steps at each end; diminishing as they descend towards the middle, or center : by the *French* called *Peronné*.

DELF, is also used in heraldry, for one of the abatements of honour; being a square in the middle of the escutcheon. A *Delf* tenne is due to him that recedes from his own challenge, or in any way departs from his parole, or word. If there be two or more *Delfs* in an escutcheon, it is then no longer an abatement; so also, if it be of metal, or charge upon, it then becomes a charge of perfect bearing.

DEMI, or **DEMY**, signified the half of a thing, like *Demy-Lion*, &c. *Colombiere* has what he calls *Croix & demy*, a cross and an half; being a shaft crossed in the upper part like the Calvary cross, and having but one arm at the lower part.

DENCHÉ, DENCHED, or **ENDENCHÉ**. See *Danché*.

DESCENT, is used to express the coming down of any thing from above. Thus a *Lyon en descent*, is a lion with his head towards one of the base points, and his heels to one of the corners in the chief; as if he were leaping from some high place.

DESHACHÉ, is when a beast has its limbs separated from its body, so as they still remain in the escutcheon, with only a small separation from their natural places.

DESPOUILLE, is the whole case, skin, or slough of a beast; with the head, feet, tail, and all appurtenances; so as being filled, or stuffed, it looks like the entire creature.

DETRENCHÉ, among the *French* heraldry, signifies a line bend-wise, which does not come from the very dexter angle, but either from some part of the upper edge, and thence falling athwart or diagonally; or from part of the dexter side. They say *Tranché, Detranché,* and *Retranché,* to denote there are two diagonal lines, making two partitions in the escutcheon, and coming from the angles, and a third from some of the other parts abovementioned.

DEVISE, is a name common to all figures, ciphers, characters, rebus's, motto's, &c. which, by their allusion to the names of persons or families, denote their qualities, nobility, or the like. *Devise*, in this sense, is of a much older standing than heraldry itself; being that which gave the first rise to armouries : thus, the Eagle was the *Devise* of the *Roman* empire; SPQR[1] was the *Devise* of the *Roman* people; and still continues to be what they call the *escutcheon of the city of Rome*.

   The first *Devises* where mere letters distributed on the borders of the liveries, housings, and banners, and, at length, on the shields. Thus the K was the *Devise* of the *French* kings of the name of *Charles*, from *Charles* V to *Charles* IX. There were also *Devises* by rebus's, equivocals, or allusions, both to names and arms. The dukes of *Greece* took for their *Devise* an A in an O, to signify *chacun A son tour*, everyone in his turn. And the house of *Senesai*, in *vertute & honore senesces*. Some that have towers in their arms, *turris mea Deus*.

   There are sixteen aenigmatical *Devises* : as that of the Golden Fleece, with *Autre n'aurai*, intimating that *Philip the Good*, who instituted that order, renounced every other woman, but *Isabella* of *Portugal*. *Devises* sometimes contain entire proverbs, as that of *Caesar Borgia, aut Caesar, aut nihil*[2].

---

[1] Senatus Populusque Romanus, *i.e.* the Senate and People of Rome
[2] "Either Caesar, or nothing"

The word *Devise* is formed from the *Latin dividere*, and was applied to things just mentioned, as well as those hereafter mentioned, by reason they served, divide, separate and distinguish persons, parties, &c. Fa. *Menestrier* observes, that there are as many different kinds of *Devises*, as there are different manners of distinguishing one another, or as there are simple figures or words, capable of expressing qualities, offices, virtues, actions, &c. of persons, and of notifying and distinguishing them from others.

DEXTER, is applied to the *right* side, as *sinister* is to the *left*.

DEXTER-*Base*, is the right side of the base.

DEXTER-*Chief*, the angle on the right side of the chief.

DEXTROCHERE, or **DESTROCHERE**, is applied to the right arm, painted in a shield, sometimes naked, sometimes clothed, or adorned with bracelet, and sometimes armed, or holding some moveable, or member used in the arms. The *Dextrochere* is sometimes placed as the crest. The word is formed from the *Latin Dextrocherium*, which signifies a bracelet worn on the right wrist, mentioned in the acts of the martyrdom of St. *Agnes*, and the life of the emperor *Maximus*.

DIADEM, is applied to certain circles, or rims, serving to bind, or inclose the crowns of sovereign princes; and to bear the globe or cross, or the flower de luce for their crest. The crowns of sovereign princes differ in this, that some are bound with a greater, and some with a lesser number of *Diadems*.

Prelates appear anciently to have worn a sort of *Diadem* : thus *Baronius*[1] writes, that St. *James* the apostle wore a gold plate on his forehead, as mark of his episcopal authority.

In blazoning, the bandages about the heads of *Moors*, on shields, is sometimes also called *Diadem*.

DIAPRÉ, or **DIAPERED**, a dividing a field into planes, or compartments, in the manner of fret-work; and filling the same with a variety of figures. This chiefly obtains on bordures, which are diapered, or fretted over; and the frets charged with things proper to bordures : as in *Tab. Herald. fig.* 18.

DIEU & *mon droit*, *q.d.* God and my right, the motto of the arms of *England*, first given by king *Richard* I to intimate that he had not held his empire in vassalage of any mortal. It was afterwards taken up by *Edward* III when he first claimed the crown of *France*; and was continued without interruption until *William* III who used the motto, *je maintiendray*; though he commanded

---

[1] Cesare Baronio, or Caesar Baronius (1538 – 1607), was an Italian Cardinal and ecclesiastical historian.

the former to be retained in the great seal. The same is to be understood of the late queen *Anne*, who used the motto *semper eadem*, which had been before used by queen *Elizabeth*.

DIFFERENCES, certain additaments to coat armour, whereby something is altered, or added, to distinguish the younger families from the elder, or shew how far they are removed from the principal house. They are called in *Latin Diminutiones*, and *Discernicula Armorium*, and by the *French Brisures*.

Of these differences, *Silvanus Morgan*[1] gives us nine, which obtain principally among us : *viz.* the *label*, which denotes the first or eldest son; the *crescent*, the second; the *mullet*, the third; the *martlet*, the fourth; the *annulet*, the fifth; the *flower de lis*, the sixth; the *rose*, the seventh; the *eight foil*, the eighth; and the *cross moline* the ninth.

Again, as the first *Differences* are single for the sons of the first house, or descent; the sons of the younger houses are differed by combining or putting the said differences upon each other. As the first *Differences* are the label, crescent, &c. for the first house, the *Difference* for the second house is the *label* on a *crescent*, for the first of that house; for the third brother of the second house, a *mullet* on a *crescent*, &c.

The original of *Differences* is controverted. *Camden* will have them to have begun about the time of king *Richard*. *Paradin*[2] assigns *Differences* wore as early as the year 870. The president *Fauchet*[3] observes *Differences* to have been hereditary in the *French* families before the time of *Louis le Gros*[4]; who came to the crown in the year 1110. *Moreau* refers them to the time of St. *Louis*, and *Lallonette, Belle-forest*, &c. to that of *Philip Augustus*. The occasion of their rise is well accounted for by *Colombiere*.

All nations, says he, prefer the eldest brothers to the younger; whence those, in a direct line, succeeding their fathers, and becoming masters of their lands, took on them their coat armour without any change or alteration; and transmitted the same again to their eldest sons : the younger brothers or bastards not being allowed to bear the same arms, without some additional mark, to distinguish them from the elder. Hence some heralds, he goes on, have endeavoured to confine them to certain fixed and determinate figures, for distinguishing the second from the first, the third from the second; and so on to the sixth : assigning the second a label, the third a bordure, the fourth an orle, the fifth a battoon, and the sixth a bend or cottice.

And the descendants of these do bear double *Differences*, or *Differences* charged on one another, *viz.* the eldest son of the second son to retain his paternal coat, with the *Difference* of the *label* of three points; the second the label of four points; the third such a *label* on a chief; the fourth a *label* charged with certain figures, as *eagles, lioncels, martlets, crescents, roses*,

---

[1] Sylvanus Morgan (1620-1693), who was an English arms-painter and author.
[2] Claude Paradin (post 1510-1573), who was a French canon and author.
[3] Claude Fauchet (1530 – 1602), who was a French historian and antiquary.
[4] Louis VI (1081 – 1137)

&c. And for the same reason the second son of the third son will bear a bordure engrailed, the third a bordure charged with bezants, or tourteaux.

But the same author judges the fixing any certain invariable *Differences* at all an abuse; by reason they may happen not to be agreeable to the paternal coat, but very much deface and blemish it. He adds, that many other figures besides those abovementioned, may be used as *Differences*; as shells, bezarits, cinque-foils, and a thousand more. Some younger families have made the *Difference* in their arms by only diminishing the ordinaries, or changing their posture; and others by only changing the metal or colour.

It must be added that the *Difference* may be of metal on metal, or colour on colour; which in other cases is false heraldry.

DIMINUTIONS, a term used by *Latin* writer for what we more usually call *Differences*, and the *French Brisures*. See *Differences*.

DISPLAYED, is understood of the position of an eagle, or other bird, when it is erect, with its wings expanded, or spread forth.

DISVELOPPED, is used much in the same sense as displayed. Thus colours, said in an army to be flying, are in heraldry said to be *disvelloped*. See *Displayed*.

DIVAL, the herb night-shade, used by such as blazon with flowers and herbs instead of colours and metals, for sable, or black.

DORMANT, is the heralds term for the posture of a lion, or other beast, born as sleeping in the coat of arms.

DOUBLE *Fiché*, or **DOUBLE** *Fichy*. A cross is denominated *double fiché*, when the extremities are point at each angle; that is, each extremity has two points : in contradistinction to fiche, where the extremity is sharpened away to one point. *Leigh*[1] calls it *double pitchy*, which seems to be a mistake. *Gibbon* expresses it by an octagonal cross, the two points whereof at each extremity are parted inwards by a small space of a line. By which it is distinguished from the cross of *Malta*; the two points whereof proceed from a third point, or acute angle between them.

DOUBLINGS, the linings of robes, or mantles of state; or of the mantlings in atchievements.

DRAGONEE. A *Lyon Dragonnee* is where the upper half resembles a Lyon; the other half going off like the hind part of a dragon. The like may be said of any other beast as well as a lyon.

---

[1] Gerard Legh (died 1563), was an English lawyer, known as a writer on heraldry.

DWAL, the herb night-shade, used by such as blazon with flowers and herbs instead of colours and metals, for sable, or black.

ℰ

EAGLET, or **EAGLON**, a diminutive of *Eagle*, properly signifying a young *Eagle*. The *Eagle* is said to prove his *Eaglets* in the brightness of the sun; if they shut their eye lids, he disowns them. In heraldry, when there are several *Eagles* on the same escutcheon, they are called *Eaglets*.

ECHIQUETTE. See *Checky*.

ECUSSON, an inescutcheon, or little escutcheon. See *Escutcheon*.

EFFARÉ, or **EFFRAYÉ**, a term applied to a beast when rearing on its hind legs as if it were affrighted.

EMBATTLED, a term in heraldry, when the out-line of any ordinary after the manner expressed in *Tab. Herald. Fig.* 56. representing the battlements of a wall or castle.

ENALURON, is used by *Guillim* to express a bordure charged with birds; as an *enaluron* of martlets, &c. But *Mackenzy*[1] charges this a mistake arising from ignorance of the *French* tongue; *enaluron* properly signifying orle, or in a manner of a bordure, and being applicable to a bearing of any thing in that form.

ENCEPPÉ, denotes chained, or girt round the middle; as is usual with monkies [sic], &c.

ENDENTED, DENTED, INDENTED. See *Indented*.

---

[1] Possibly Sir George Mackenzie of Rosehaugh (c. 1636 – 1691), who was a Scottish lawyer, Lord Advocate, essayist and legal writer.

ENDENTED is also applied to a fess, pale, and other triangular pieces, when divided alternately between two different colours. Coupé, or *endented* or with azure.

ENDORSE, an ordinary containing the eighth part of a pale. This, *Leigh* says, is never used but when a pale is between two such : others hold, that an *endorse* may be bore between birds, fishes, beasts, &c. Sir. *J. Ferne*[1] adds, that it shews the same coat has been two coats, and afterwards conjoined in one escutcheon, for some mystery of arms. He bears azure an *endorse* argent. *Tab. Herald. fig.* 56. No. 2

ENDORSED, ENDOSSÉ, is where things are bore back to back.

ENGRAILED, or **INGRAILED**, is when a thing is represented with its edges ragged, or notched circularly, as if broke by something falling on it. See *Tab. Herald. fig.* 56. It differs from *indented*, in that the breaches are all in straight lines; but here semi-circular : and from *invected*, in that the points of the little arches are turned inwards towards the middle of the field; which in *invected* are turned outwards. *Spelman* expresses it in *Latin* by *imbricatus*, others by *ingrediatus*, and others by *striatus*.

ENGUISSE, is applied to the great mouth of a hunting horn, when it has a rim of a different colour from the horn itself.

ENTE, literally implies engrafted; and is used by the foreign heralds to express a method of marshaling, little known among us. Yet we have in instance of it in the fourth grand quarter of his majesty's royal ensign; whose blazon is, *Brunwic* and *Lunenburgh* impaled with ancient *Saxony*, *enté in pointe*.

ENTOYER, or **ENTOIRE**, is used to express a bordure charged entirely without life.

ENVIRONNE, is when a lion, or other figure, is *environed*, or encompassed round with other things. *Environné* with so many bezants, &c.

ENURNY is the herald's term for the bordure of a coat of arms being charged with any kind of beasts.

EQUIPPÉ, expresses a cavalier equipped, *i.e.* armed at all points.

---

[1] Sir John Ferne (c. 1560 – 1609), was a writer on heraldry, a genealogist, and a lawyer.

ERASED, expresses any thing violently torn off from its proper place. It is used on contradistinction to *couped*, which signifies a thing clean cut off. The family of *Card* bears ermine, a demi-lion rampant erased, azure, &c.

ERMINE, or **ERMINE**, a white field, or fur, powdered, or interspersed with black spots. It is supposed to represent the skin of an animal of the same denomination; which some will have a water-rat, others a sort of weazle, and others an *Armenian* mouse. In effect, there is no animal that naturally corresponds to the herald's ermine.

The animal is milk white; and so far is it from spots, that the tradition has it, he will rather die, or be taken, than sully its whiteness. Whence its symbolical use. But white skins have for many ages been used for the linings of the robes of magistrates and great men; the furriers, at length, to add to their beauty, used to sew bits of the black tails of those creatures upon the white skins; to render them more conspicuous. Which alteration was introduced into heraldry. See *Tab. Herald. fig.* 57.

The sable spots in ermine are not of any determinable number, but may be more or less, at the pleasure of the painter or furrier.

ERMINÉ. A *Cross erminé*, is a cross composed of four *ermine* spots, placed in the figure represented *Tab. Herald. fig.* 58. It must be observed, that the colours in such arms are not to be expressed; by reason, neither the cross, nor the arms, can be of any colour but white and black. *Colombiere* blazons it *quatre queurs d'ermine en croix*. The editor of *Guillim* describes it thus; a cross of four *ermines*; or, more properly, of four *ermine* spots in a cross. It is the coat of *Hurston* in *Cheshire*.

ERMINES, is used by some *English* writers, for the reverse of *ermine*, i.e. for white spots on a black field : but on what foundation nobody can tell; for the *French*, from whom we have our heraldry, have no such term; but call this black powdered with white, *contre-ermine*; as denoting the counter or reverse of *ermine*; which is white powdered with black. See *Tab. Herald. fig.* 59.

ERMINITES, should seem a diminutive of *ermines*, and naturally to signify little *ermines*; but it is otherwise. *Erminites* expresses a white field powdered with black; only every spot has a little red hair therein. Some authors use the word *Erminites* for a yellow field powdered with black; which the French express much better by *or semé ermines de sable*.

ESCARTELÉ, *quartered*, or *quarterly*. See *Quartering* and *Quarterly*.

ESCLATTÉ, is applied to a thing not violently broke. Thus a bend, or other partition, *esclatté*, is represented torn or broke off like a shield shattered with a stroke of a battle ax.

ESCROL, or **SCROLL**, a long slip, as it were, of parchment, or paper, whereon a motto is placed. *Leigh* observes, that no person, under the degree of knight, might, long after king *Henry* I placed his crest on a wreath, as is now usually done, but only on an *escrol*.

ESCUTCHEON, or **SCUTCHEON**, the shield, or coat, wherein the bearing, or arms of any person is represented. The *escutcheon* is of a square figure, excepting the bottom part, which is usually a little rounded, ending in a point in the middle. See *Tab. Herald. fig.* 38.

Till within a few hundred years, the escutcheons of the *French* and *English* were triangular : those of the *Spaniards* are still quite round at the bottom without any point : and those of the *Germans* in form of cartoozes. The ancient *escutcheons* were generally couched or inclined; and they only began to place them upright, when crowns, &c. were put over them by way of crest.

In *France escusson, escutcheon*, was formerly restrained to a shield, or coat, pointed at bottom; by which it was distinguished from the *escu*, which was quite square, and was only allowed to be bore by the counts and viscounts. Those of inferior quality were confined to the *escusson*, or pointed *escu*.

The several parts and points of an escutcheon have their several names : the point A, for instance is the *dexter chief point*; B the *middle chief*; and C the *sinister chief point*; D is the *honour point*; E the *fess point*; F the *nombril point*; G the *dexter base*; H the *middle*; I the *sinister base*.

The *escutcheon* is diversely denominated according to its division. It is called *dextered* when the perpendicular line that divides it is to the right of a third part of the *escutcheon*; *sinistered*, when on the left : *tierced in pale* when this line is double, and divides the whole *escutcheon* into three equal parts : *paled* when increased to the number of six, eight or ten. A horizontal line makes the *chief* when at one third part from the top; the *plein* when at one third part from the bottom : and when double, in the middle, at an equal distance from both extremes, it makes the *fess*, and *tierced in fess* : when it is multiplied it denominates it *fessed* : when there are eight or ten equal spaces, *burellé* : a diagonal from the dexter point of the chief to the sinister of the base makes it *tranche*; the contrary, *doublé*. If it doubled at equal distances, the first makes, *barré* or *tierce in bar* : increasing the number of the first makes *bandé* and *cotticé*; and increasing that of the second *barré* and *traversé*.

The word *escutcheon* is formed of the *French escusson*, and that from the *Latin scutum*, shield; which was the place arms were originally bore on, before ever they came on banners; and still, wherever they are placed, it is something representing the form of a shield. The *Latin scutum*, no doubt came originally from the *Greek* σκυτος, leather, wherewith the shields were usually covered.

ESCUTCHEON *of pretence*, is an *inescutcheon*, or little *escutcheon*, which a man, who has married an heiress, and has issue by her, may bear over his own coat of arms; and in it the arms of his wife : and the surviving issue will bear both arms quarterly. See *Tab. Herald. fig.* 63.

ESSORANT, a term used to express a bird standing in the ground with the wings expanded, as if it had been wet, and were drying itself.

ESTETÉ, is used by the *French* to signify a beast whose head has been, as it were, torn off by force; and consequently the neck left rough and rugged; in contra-distinction to *dessait*, or *decapité*, where the neck is smooth; as if the head had been cut off.

ESTOILÉ. A *Cross estoilé*, is a star with only four long rays, in manner of a cross; and accordingly broad in the centre, and terminating in sharp points.

F

FAILLIS, a *French* term denoting some failure or flaw in an ordinary, as if it were broke, and a splinter taken from it.

FALSE *arms*, are those wherein the fundamental rules of the art are not observed; as if metal be put on metal, or colour on colour, &c.

FENDUE *en pal*, a *French* phrase applied to a cross, to denote it cloven down from top to bottom, and the parts set at some distance from one another.

FER *de fourchette, Croix a fer de fourchette*, is a cross having a forked iron at each end, like that formerly used by soldiers to rest their muskets on; by which it is distinguished from the *cross fourché*; the ends whereof turn forked : whereas in this the fork is fixed on the square end; as represented in *Tab. Herald. fig.* 20.

FER *de Moulin*, *q.d.* iron of the mill, is a bearing in heraldry; supposed to represent the iron-ink, or ink of the mill, which sustains the moving mill-stone. See a representation of it in *Tab. Herald. fig.* 21.

FESSE, one of the nine honourable ordinaries of the escutcheon, which it divides horizontally in the middle, and separates the chief from the point. It is supposed to represent a broad girdle, or belt of honour which knights at arms were anciently girded withal. It possesses the centre of the escutcheon, and contains in breadth one third part thereof. Thus, he beareth azure, a *Fesse* or, by the name of *Eliott*. See *Tab. Herald. fig.* 22. When the *Fesse* takes up less than its proper breadth, it is called a *bar*.

FESSE-*point*, is the exact centre of the escutcheon. It is thus called from being the point through which the *Fesse* line is drawn from the two sides; and accordingly divides the escutcheon into two equal parts, when the escutcheon is parted *per-Fesse*.

FESSE-*ways*, or *in Fesse*, denotes things born after the manner of a *Fesse*; *i.e.* in a line or range, a-cross the middle of the shield, from side to side through the *Fesse* point; which the *French* call *en Fesse*.

Party per **FESSE**, implies parted a-cross the middle of the shield from side to side, through the *Fesse* point. This the *French* express by one word, *coupé*. See *Couped*.

FEUILLE *de scie*, expresses that an ordinary, as a fesse, pale, or the like, is indented only on one side; in regard it then looks like the leaf of a saw, as the *French* phrase imports.

FICHE. See *Fitchee*.

FIELD, is the surface of face of the shield, or escutcheon; thus called, as containing the atchievements anciently acquired in the *field* of battle. The *field* is the ground whereon the colours, bearings, metals, furs, colours, &c. are represented. In blazoning a coat, we always begin with the *field* : he bears sable, &c. Among the more modern heralds, *field* is less frequently used than shield or escutcheon.

FIGURE, a bearing in a shield, representing or resembling a human face; as a sun, a wind, an angel, &c.

FILE, or *label*, as being represented in *Tab. Herald. fig.* 23. though sometimes of more and sometimes of fewer points, being the difference or distinction of a second son. It is sometimes also born as a charge in coat-armour, of which *Guillim* gives many instances : but it is oftener the difference or mark of distinction, which the elder brother bears in his coat, during his father's life. Some distinguish *File* and label, calling the *File* the upper horizontal line, and the label the points which issue from it.

FILLET, *Teniola*, a kind of orle, or bordure, containing only a third or fourth part of the breadth of the common bordure. It is supposed to be withdrawn inwards; and is of a different colour from the field. It runs quite around, near the edge, as a lace over a cloak.

FILLET, is also used for an ordinary drawn like the bar, from the sinister side of the chief a-cross the shield; in manner of a scarf, : tho' it is sometimes also seen in the situation of a bend, fesse, cross, &c. According to *Guillim* the *Fillet* is the fourth part of the chief; and placed in the chief point of the escutcheon.

FIMBRIATED, a term in heraldry signifying that an ordinary is edged round with another of a different colour. Thus, he beareth or, a cross patee gules *fimbriated* sable.

FISHES, are of themselves of less esteem in a coat-amour, than beasts or fowls, as being posterior thereto in the order of creation : but they sometimes become dignified by the person or families who bear them, as to be preferable to many birds and beasts.

FITCHEE, or **FICHEE**, is when the lower part of any cross is sharpened to a point, fit to fix into the ground. Thus, he bears azure, a cross potent *Fitchee*. See *Tab. Herald. fig.* 24. The origin hereof *Mackenzy* ascribes to the primitive Christians, who used to carry their crosses with them, wherever they went; and when the stopped in any place in a journey, fixed the in the ground,

FLANCH, FLANQUE, or **FLASQUE**, an ordinary in heraldry, formed by an arched line, which begins at the corners of the chief, and ends in the base of the escutcheon. He beareth ermin, two *Flanches* vert. See *Tab. Herald. fig.* 25. *Flanches* are born by pairs. *Leigh* makes *Flanque* and *Flasque* two distinct bearings, whereof the former is bent in than the latter; but *Gibbon* judiciously makes them but one, which he calls *Flanque*.

FLANKED, FLANQUE, is used by the *French* heralds, to express our party per salteer; that is, when the field is divided into four parts, after the manner of an X. Though *Colombiere* uses the term in another sense, which appears more natural, *viz.* for the taking of flanches, or rounding sections out of the sides of the escutcheon; the first from the angles of it, the latter in straight lines, forming an angle at the fesse, without making any saltier.

FLORY, FLOWERY, FLEURY, FLORETTEE, FLEUR-DE-LISSE, &c. terms in heraldry, used when the outlines of any ordinary are drawn as if trimmed with, or in the form of, flowers, lilies, flowers-de-luces, &c.

FLOWER-DE-LUCE, FLEUR DE LIS, is a bearing anciently of great dignity; being reputed the noblest of all flowers, and as such having been in all ages the charge of the royal escutcheon of the kings of *France*; though tract of time has made the bearing thereof more vulgar. In some coats it is bore single; in others, triple; in others it is semée, seeded all over the escutcheon.

FORMÉ, or **FORMY**. A *Cross Formé*, or *Formy*, is a cross narrow in the centre, and broad at the extremes; so called by *Leigh* and *Morgan*; though most other authors call it *Patee*. See *Patee*.

FOURCHEE, or **FOURCHY**. A *Cross fourchee* is that forked at the ends. *Upton* rather represents it as anchored, the extremities turning in a circular manner to sharp points; whereas the true *cross fourchee*, *i.e.* forked, has its forks composed of straight lines and blunt ends. See *Tab. Herald. fig.* 33.

FRET, or **FRETTE**, is a bearing consisting of six bars, crossed and interlaced *fret-wise*; as in *Tab. Herald. fig.* 39. *Guillim* derives the word from the *French rett*, net; but the reader will easily furnish himself with a better etymology from the word *Fret* in architecture.When it consists of more than six pieces, the number must be specified.

He bears diamond a *Fret* topaz : the coat armour formerly of the lord *Maltrevers*, and now quartered by the duke of *Norfolk*.

Some call this the *true Lovers Knot*; others, *Harrington's Knot*, because it is their arms, and *Nodo firmo*, the motto. *Gibbon* is calling it *Heraldorum nodus amatorius*.

FRETTY, or **FRETTE**, is where there are divers bars laid a-cross each other. Fretty is of six, eight or more pieces. Azure, *Fretty* of eight pieces or : the coat of lord *Willoughby*[1].

FURCHE, a cross in the form represented in *Tab. Herald. fig.* 41.

FURR, a representation of the skins of certain wild beasts, seen, both in the doublings of the mantles of coat amour, and in the armour itself. The heralds use two metals, five colours, and two *Furrs*, or hairy skins, *viz.* ermine and vair.

The origins of these *Furrs*, *Mackenzy* ascribes to the shield's being anciently covered with skins, which skins or coverings were afterwards represented in the shields : a more probable derivation, in our opinion, than to say they were placed on shields, because they had been wore in mantles and garments.

Furrs either consist of one colour, which is white; or more than one; and these either two, or more than two. *Furrs* of two colours are either ermine being white with black spots; ermines, black with white spots; erminois, whose ground is yellow; or pean, which is black powdered with yellow. *Furrs* of more than two colours are called vair. See *Vair* and *Vairy*.

FUSIL, by the *French* called *Fusee*, *q.d.* a spindle; is a bearing of a rhomboidal figure, more slender than the lozenge; its upper and lower angles being more acute than the two middle ones. See *Tab. Herald. fig.* 42.

FUSILY, or **FUSILÉ**, is when a field or ordinary is entirely covered over, or divided into *Fusils*.

---

[1] Probably Francis Willoughby, 5th Baron Willoughby of Parham (ca. 1614 – 1666), who was an English peer of the House of Lords.

G

GARTER, is a term in heraldry, signifying moiety, or half, of a bend.

GEMELLES, a bearing of bars by pairs, or couples, in a coat of arms. He beareth gules on a chevron argent, three bars *gemelles* sable, by the name of *Throgmorton*.

GIRON, or **GUIRON**, a triangular figure, having a long sharp point, not unlike a wedge, terminating in the centre of the escutcheon. When a coat has six, eight, or ten of these *girons*, meeting or centering in the middle of the coat, it is said to be *gironné* or *girony*.

The word is *French* and literally signifies the *gremiom*, or lap; by reason, in sitting, the knees being supposed somewhat asunder, the two thighs, together with a line imagined to pass from one knee to the other, for a figure somewhat similar hereto.

GIRONNÉ, or **GIRONY**, is when a shield or coat is divided into several *girons*, which are alternately colour and metal, See *Tab. Herald. fig.* 63. Which his blazoned *gironné* of six argent and sable.

When there are eight pieces or *girons*, it is absolutely said to be *gironné*; when there are more or fewer the number is to be expressed. *Gironné* of four, of fourteen, &c.

Some, instead of *gironné*, say *parti, coupé tranché*, and *taillé*, by reason the *girons* are formed by such divisions of the field. Four *girons* form a salteer and eight a cross.

GOLPS, are roundels, or tourteaux of a purple colour.

GORE, one of the regular abatements, used, according to *Guillim*, to denote a coward. It consists of two arches, or curve lines, drawn from the sinister chief, the other from the sinister base, and meeting in an acute angle at the middle of the fess-point; as represented in *Tab. Herald. fig.* 64.

GORGED, is when a crown, coronet, or the like thing is bore about the neck of a lion, swan, &c. In that case they say, the lion or cygnet is *gorged* with a ducal coronet, &c. *Gorged* is also used when the gorge, or neck, of a peacock, swan, or the like bird, is of a different colour or metal from the rest.

GROANING, a term used for the cry or noise of a buck.

The **GROUND** *of a shield*, or escutcheon, is properly called the field.

GARDANT, a term applied to a beast, when born in a coat of arms, full faced, or with his face turned towards the spectator, and thus appearing in a posture of guard and defence.

GUSSET, one of the abatements of honour, appropriated to lascivious, effeminate, or wanton persons. It is formed of a line drawn from the dexter or sinister angle of the chief, and descending diagonally to the chief point; from whence another line falls perpendicularly upon the base; as represented in *Tab. Herald. fig.* 65.

GUTTY, or **GUTTÉ**, is when a thing is represented as charged or sprinkled with drops. In blazon the colour of the drops is to be named : thus, *gutty* of sable, of gules, &c. Some authors will have red drops called *gutty de sang*, or drops of blood; black ones, *gutty de poix*, of pitch; white, *gutty d'eau*, of water, &c.

GUZES, roundels of sanguine or murray colour.

H

HANDS, are born in a coat armour, dexter and sinister; that is, right and left; expanded or open, and after other manners. Azure a dexter *hand* couped at the wrist, and extended in pale argent; is born by the name of *Brome*. Argent, three sinister *hands*, couped at the wrist, gules, by the name of *Maynard*. Knights baronets are to bear in a canton, or in an escutcheon, which they please, the arms of *Ulster*, *viz*. in a field argent, a sinister *hand* couped at the writs, gules.

HATCHINGS are of great use in heraldry, to distinguish the several colours of an escutcheon, without its being illumined. The first kind of *hatching* in pale, from top to bottom, signifies *gules*, or *red*. The second in fess, across the coat, *azure*, or *blue*.

Hatching in pale, *counter-hatching* in fess, signifies sable, or black. *Hatching* in bend, from right to left, signifies *green*; and that in bars, from left to right, *purple*. When the coat is only dotted, it is supposed to be *or*; and when quite bar, or white, *argent*.

The invention is commonly ascribe to F. *Pietra Sancta[1]*; thought the Sieur *de la Colombiere* has disputed his title to it.

HATCHMENT, the marshaling of several coats of arms in an escutcheon.

HATCHMENT is also a popular name for an atchievement.

HELMET, or **HELM**, an ancient armour of defence, wore by the cavaliers both in war and tournaments; and still used by way or crest, or ornament, over the shield or coat of arms. The *helmet* is known by divers other names *cask*, *head-piece*, *steel-cap*, &c. The *helmet* covered the head and face, only leaving an aperture about the eyes, secured by bars, which served as a visor.

The *helmet* is bore in armoury as a mark of nobility; and by the different circumstances of the bearing of the *helmet*, are the different degrees of nobility indicated. In *France*, where all our heraldry originally came, the following rules obtain.

A person newly ennobled, or made a gentleman, bears over his escutcheon a helmet of bright iron, or steel, in profile, or standing sideways; the visor quite closed. A gentleman of three descents bears it a little open, but still in profile, shewing three bars of the visor. Ancient knights, &c. have it in profile but showing five bars; the edges of silver.

---

[1] Silvester Petra Sancta (1590 – 1647), was an Italian Jesuit and heraldist.

A baron's *helmet* is of silver, the edges gold; with seven bars, neither quite in profile, nor yet in front; with a coronet over it, adorned with pearls. Viscounts and earls formerly bore a silver *helmet*, with gold edges; its position like the former : but now they bear it quite fronting with a coronet over it. Marquises bear a silver *helmet*, damasked, fronting; with eleven bars, and their coronet. Dukes and princes have their *helmet*, damasked, fronting, the visor almost open, without bars; with their coronets over them.

Lastly, the *helmets* of kings and princes are all of gold, damasked, full fronting, and the visor quite open, and without bars. The *helmets* of bastards are to be turned to the left to denote their bastardy.

Among the *English* heralds these laws are of late somewhat varied. *Leigh* will have the *helmet* in profile, and closed, to belong to knights; but all other authors give it to esquires and gentlemen.

To a knight they assign the *helmet* standing right forward, and the bearer a little open. The *helmet* in profile, or posited sideways, and open with bars, belongs to a nobleman, under the condition of a duke. The *helmet* right forward, open, with many bars, is assigned to dukes princes, and kings.

Those turned sideways are supposed to be giving ear to the commands of their superiors; and those right forwards to be giving commands with absolute authority.

Commonly there is but one *helmet* in a shield; but sometimes two or three; if there be two, they must be placed facing each other; if three, the two extremes must be looking towards that in the middle.

HERALD, an officer in arms, anciently of great repute, and possessed of several considerable functions, rights, and privileges.

The word *Herald*, according to *Du Cange*[1], comes from the *German heer*, army, and *ald*, servant; because chiefly serving in the army. Others will have the two words signify *champion of the army*; in allusion to their office of denouncing war, proclaiming peace, &c. *Du Cange* adds, that they were called *clarigarii*, as well as *heralds*. *Borel*[2] derives the word from the *Latin herus*, master, *q.d.* one coming from his master. Others from *herhaut*, *q.d.* high lord : others from *herold*, which is the same with *dominus veteranus* : and others, lastly, from *heer*, master, or army, and *hold*, *q.d.* bound to his lord, or the army.

The origins of *heralds* is very ancient. *Stentor* is represented by *Homer* as herald of the *Greeks*, who had a voice louder than fifty men. The *Greeks* called them κηρυχες and ειρηνοφολακς, and the *Romans*, *feciales*. The *Romans* had a college of *heralds*, appointed to decide whether a war were just or unjust; and to prevent its coming to open hostilities, till all means had been attempted for deciding the difference in a pacific way.

---

[1] Charles du Fresne, sieur du Cange or Ducange (1610 – 1688), was a French philologist and historian.
[2] Possibly Pierre Borel (ca. 1620 – 1671), who was a French chemist, physician, and botanist.

Heralds, or *heralds at arms*, have formerly been denominated *dukes at arms*, because properly belonging to dukes; as kings at arms, to kings.

In *England* we have six *heralds, viz.* 1° *Richmond*, 2° *Lancaster*, 3° *Chester*, 4° *Windsor*, 5° *Somerset*, 6° *York*. To which may be added a seventh, *Brunswick herald*, erected by king *George* I. Their office is to wait at court, to attend public solemnities, proclaim war and peace, look to the regulation of the bearings of arms, search pedigrees, &c.

They were formerly created and christened by the king, who slowly pouring a gold cup of wine on their head, gave them their *herald's* name. Now it is done by the earl-marshal. They could not arrive at the dignity of *herald*, without having been seven years poursuivant : nor could they quit the function of *herald*, but to be made king at arms.

Their principal employment was to compose, or make out coats of arms, genealogies, and titles of nobility. They were the superintendents of military exploits, and the conservators of the honours of war. They had the right to take away the arms of such as for cowardice, treason, &c. deserved to be degraded. They had a commission to examine and correct the vices and disorders of the nobles, and to exclude them from jousts, tournament, &c. to them belonged the correcting of all usurpations and abuses relating to crowns, coronets, casks, crests, supporters, &c. They took cognizance of all differences among the noble, with respect to their bearings, the antiquity of their families, precedence, &c.

They went into the countries to search into the grounds and pretensions of nobility; and had a right to open all libraries, and to command all the old charters and instruments in the archives to be shewn them. They had admission into all foreign courts, where they were commissioned to proclaim war and peace; and their persons were held sacred, as those of ambassadors. To them it belonged to make publication of jousts and tournaments; to call the people to them; to signify the cartels; to mark the ground, lift, or place of duel; to see fair play observed; and to divide the sun between the two parties.

In the army, they advertised the cavaliers and captains of the day of battle, and assisted therein before the standard; retiring after the first onset to some place of eminence, there to observe who behaved best, and to give a faithful report thereof to the king. They numbered the dead, relieved the ensigns, re-demanded prisoners, summoned places to surrender, and in capitulations walked before the governour of the place, to secure and warrant his person. They were the principal arbitrators of the distribution of the spoils of the vanquished, and of military rewards. They published victories; and gave notifications thereof to foreign courts. They convened the states of the kingdom, assisted at royal marriages, and frequently made the first demand; officiated at solemn feasts, &c.

The modern *heralds, i.e.* those we properly call *heralds* have lost a good deal of the distinction and offices of the ancient ones. What relates to the making out arms, the rectifying of abuses therein, &c. is chiefly committed to the kings at arms.

And in the army, drums and trumpets have succeeded to the function of *heralds*, being sent by the generals on the same errands; and on that account enjoying the same rights and privileges. Their persons are under the protection of the law of nations, when they bear the marks of their office publickly, *i.e.* the trumpeter, his trumpet, and the drummer, his drum; in the same manner as the *herald* his coat.

The *heralds*, with the kings at arms, and the four poursuivant, are a college, or corporation; erected into such by charter of *Richard* III, who granted them divers privileges, as to be free from subsidies, tolls, and all troublesome offices.

HERALDRY, the art of armoury and blazoning, or the knowledge of what relates to the bearing of arms, and the laws and regulations thereof. *Heraldry* likewise comprehends what relates to the marshaling of solemn cavalcades, processions and other ceremonies at coronations, installments, creations of peers, nuptials, funerals, &c.

HONOUR *Point*, is that next above the centre of the escutcheon; dividing the upper part into two equal portions.

HONOURABLE, or **HONORABLE** *Ordinaries*, are the principal ordinaries or bearings, which, when in their full extent, may possess one third of the field. Some only allow of nine, *viz.* the *cross, chief, pale, bend, fesse, chevron, salteer, giron,* and *escutcheon*; others add more, *viz.*, the *bar, bordure,* &c. See each under its proper article.

[**HUMETTY**, is a term applied to certain ordinaries instead of couped, which is applied to charges, and especially those of animals. Applied to the fesse and the bar, *humetty* signifies that both ends are cut off so as not to reach to the edge of the shield. When applied to crosses and saltiers, all four ends are so treated; and when there is more than one of either of these in the same shield they are to be drawn *humetty*, though it be not expressed. It does not appear that a bend is ever *humetty*, and the single bendlet so treated would be blazoned a baton, *q.v.* nor has any example been observed of a pale or pile so blazoned; the chevron and the pallet are sometimes couped, but the term *humetty* seems not to be applied to them.]

HURTS, by some wrote *Heurts*, and by others *Huerts*, are azure or blue roundels. The *English* heralds distinguish between the colours of roundels, and give them different names agreeable thereto : those of other nations content themselves to call these *torteaux d'azure*; and in other cases, only add the respective to the term *torteaux*. But these being blue, some will have them signifying bruises or contusions in the flesh, which often turn to that colour; others suppose them wortle berries.

J

IMPALED, is understood of a shield party per pale, or divided into halves by a line drawn palewise through the middle, from the top to the bottom. When the coats of arms of man and his wife, who is not an heiress, are born in the same escutcheon, they must be *impaled*, or marshaled in pale, *i.e.* the husband's on the right side, and the wife's on the left; and this the heralds call *baron et feme*, two coats impaled.

[**INCROISSANT**. The crescent is sometimes montant, that is, its points look towards the top of the chief, which is its most ordinary representation ; and hence some contend that the crescent, absolutely so called, implies that situation; though other authors blazon it montant when the horns are towards the dexter side of the escutcheon, in which position others call it *incroissant*.]

INDENTED, INDENTEE, is when the out-line of a bordure, ordinary, &.c is notched in form of teeth of a saw.

INESCUTCHEON, a small escutcheon born in a larger one, as part of some other coat. He beareth ermin, an *inescutcheon* gules. This is also sometimes called an *escutcheon of pretence*. He who marries an heiress bears here coat of arms in an *inescutcheon*, or *escutcheon of pretence*, in the middle of the coat.

INVECTED, denotes a thing fluted or furrowed. *Invected* is the just reverse of *engrailed*, in which the points are turned outward to the field : whereas in *invected* they are turned inwards to the ordinary.

J

JESSANT, is applied to a flower-de-luce, or the like figure, seeming to spring, or shoot out of some other charge. He bears sable, three leopard heads *jessant*, flowers-de-lys, or. The word is formed from the obsolete *French jesser*, to rise or spring out.

L

LABEL, a kind of addition to the arms of a younger brother, especially the second to distinguish him from the first. The *label* is esteemed the most honourable of all differences; and is formed by a fillet, usually placed in the middle, and along the chief of the coat, without touching its extremities. Its breadth ought to be a ninth part of the chief. It is adorned with pendants somewhat like the drops under the trigliphs in the Doric freeze. When there are above three pendants, the number must be specified in blazoning. There are sometimes six.

LIONCELES, a term for lions when there are more than two of them born in any coat of arms, and no ordinary between them.

M

MANTLE, or **MANTLING**, that appearance of folding of cloth, flourishing, or drapery, that is in any atchievement, drawn about the coat of arms. It is supposed originally to have been the representation of a *Mantle*, or military habit worn by ancient cavaliers over their armour, to prevent it from rust; or, as others hold, a short covering worn over the helmet; which in after-times was lengthened, and made to hang from the helmet below the whole shield. See *Tab. Herald. fig.* 29. The *Mantle* in blazon is always said to be doubled, that is, lined throughout with one of the furs, as ermin, pean, vairy, &c.

MASRSHALLING *a Coat*, signifies the due and proper joining of several coats of arms belonging to distinct families in one and the same shield or escutcheon; together with their ornaments, parts, and appurtenances.

MASCLE, or **MACLE**, a bearing inform of a lozenge, and voided of the field, that is, its inner part being cut out. See *Tab. Herald. fig.* 34. According to *Guillim*, the *Mascle* represents the mesh of a net, and it an honourable bearing. It only differs from a lozenge by being voided. He bears gules, a chevron ermin, between three *Mascles* argent, by the name of *Belgrave*.

MAUNCH, the figure of an ancient sleeve of a coat, so called by the heralds; and is born in many gentleman's escutcheons : as in the earl of *Huntingdon's*. See *Tab. Herald. fig.* 40.

METAL. There are two *metals* used in heraldry, by way of colours, *viz.* gold and silver; in blazon called *or* and *argent*. In the common painting of arms, these metals are represented as yellow and white, which are the natural colour of those *metals*. In engraving, gold is expressed by dotting the coat, &c. all over; silver, by leaving it quite blank.

MOLINÉ. A *Cross moliné* is that which turns around both ways at all its extremities, though not so wide or sharp as that said to be *anchored*. In *Upton*, the points are all cut off, which makes it very different from the cross anchored. See *Fer de moulin*.

[**MONTANT**, is used in heraldry, to denote that the horns of the half-moon are turned upward, *i.e.* toward the chief of the escutcheon.]

MULLET, or **MOLLET**, a bearing in form of a flat, or rather of the rowel of a spur, which it originally represented. The *mullet* has but five points, when there are six it is called a *star*. Though others make this difference, that the *mullet* is, or ought to be, always pierced, which a star is not. See *Tab. Herald. fig.* 71.

The mullet is usually the difference or distinguishing mark for the fourth son, or third brother, or house. Though it is not often born alone as coat armour : thus Ruby on a chief pearl, two *mullets* diamond, was the coat of the famous lord *Verulam*, first Sir *Francis Bacon*.

MURREY, a kind of purple colour, called also *sanguine*.

𝕹

NAIANT, or **NATANT**, *q.d.* swimming; a term in heraldry, used in the blazoning of fishes, when drawn in an horizontal posture, fess-wise, or transversely, a-cross the escutcheon; that being their swimming postures.

NAISSANT, is applied to a lion, or other animal, showing only the head, shoulders, fore-feet, and legs, with the tip of the tail; the rest of the body being hid under the field, or some charge or ordinary thereon; from which it appears to be issuing or arising. See *Tab. Herald. fig.* 28.

Naissant differs from *issuant*, in that the animal in the former case issues out of the middle, and the latter at the bottom of the field, or charge. F. *Menestrier* says, *naissant* is only used for animals, which shew the bare head as arising out of the extremity of the chief, or from above the fesse.

NORROY, *North Roy*, *q.d.* northern king; the title of the third kings at arms, or provincial heralds. His jurisdiction lies on the north side of *Trent*, whence his name; as *Clarencieux* on the south.

NOWED, *Nowe*, *i.e.* knotted; is applied to the tails of such creatures as are very long, and sometimes represented in coat armour as if tied up in a knot.

OGRESSES, or **AGRESSES**. See *Pellets.*

ONDEE, or **ONDÉ**. See *Wavy.*

ONGLEE, or **ONGLE**, is used by the *French* heralds to denote the talons or claws of beasts or birds when of a different colour from the body.

OR, yellow, or the colour of gold. Without this or argent there can be no good armoury. In coats of nobles, it is called *topaz*; and in those of sovereign prices, *sol*. It is represented in engraving by small points, or dots, all over the field, or bearing. See *Tab. Herald. fig.* 72. It is accounted the symbol of wisdom, temperance, faith, force, constancy, &c.

ORLE, is an ordinary in form of a fillet, drawn round the shield, near the edge or extremity thereof, leaving the field vacant in the middle. Its breadth is but half that of the tressure or bordure, which contains a sixth part of the shield; the *orle* only a twelfth : add that the *orle* is its own breadth distant from the edge of a shield; whereas the bordure comes to the edge itself.

There is sometimes one *orle*, sometimes two, sometimes three. When there are three or more they take up the whole shield. It is sometimes born flory, or counterflory, like the tressure.

The form of the *orle* is the same with that of the shield; whence it resembles an inescutcheon : as represented in *Tab. Herald. fig.* 73.

If a round of martlets, cinquefoils, &c. be placed about any ordinary, in manner of an *orle*, they are said to be *en orle*, or *orle-wise*.

ℙ

PALE, is one of the honourable ordinaries in an escutcheon; being the representation of a *pale* or stake placed upright; and comprehending the whole height of the coat, from the top of the chief to the point.

Du Cange derives the name from the *Latin* name, *palla*, or hanging, or piece of tapestry; the ancients gave the name *pales* to the hangings or linings of walls : thus a chamber was said to be *paled* with cloth of gold, with silk, &c. as consisting of bands or stuffs of two colours. Hence also the original of the word *pale*, a stake, &c. The arms of *Arragon* are *paled* or, and gules.

When the *pale* is single it is to contain one third of the breadth of the shield. When there are several, more properly called *pallets*, they are proportioned so, as to take up two fifths of the shield; and three take up three sevenths; and in those cases the number of pieces is specified as well as that of those they are charged withal, &c.

Pales are bore various ways, as *wavy*, *crenelli*, *faillis*, *indented*, *ingrailed*, &c. There are also *cometed* and *flaming pales*, which are pointed, sometimes waved, &c.

PALED, PALÉ. A coat is said to be *paled* when it is equally charged with *pales* of metal and colour. It is *counter-paled* when it is cut, and the two demi-*pales* of the chief, though of colours the same with those of the point, yet differ in the place where they meet; so as if the first of the chief be metal, that corresponding to it, underneath, is of colour. The coat is said to be *palisse* when the *pales* are pointed like those used in the defence of places.

In **PALE**, is applied to things born one above another in manner of a *pale*.

Party per **PALE**, is when the shield is divided by a single line through the middle from top to bottom. See *Party* and *Paly*.

PALISSÉ, a range of *palisades* before a fortification on a fesse, rising up considerable height and pointed atop, with the field appearing through them. See *Tab. Herald. fig.* 31.

PALL, denotes a kind of cross, representing the *pallium*, or archiepiscopal ornament sent from *Rome* to metropolitans. See its figure in *Tab. Herald. fig.* 32. Which is blazoned thus : He beareth gules, a cross *pall* argent.

PALLET, is the moiety, or half of the pale; or a small pale half the breadth of a usual one. The *pallet* must never be charged with any thing quick or dead, neither can it be divided into two equal parts; but it may be into four; for one fourth part of the *pallet*, or two eighth parts of the pale, is called an *endorse*. If the pale be on any beast, they say, the beast is *debruised* with the pale; but if the beast be upon the pale, they say he is *supported* by it.

PALY, or **PALÉ**. When an escutcheon is divided into six, eight, or ten divisions pale-wide, *i.e.* by perpendicular lines drawn from top to bottom : it is blazoned *paly* of six, eight, or ten, &c. pieces. If the number be odd, the shield is first named, and the number of the pales specified. The like is also to be understood of barry and bendy.

PALY-BENDY is when a coat is divided both pale- and bend-wise. In *paly-bendy* the field is divided by perpendicular lines which is called *paly*; and then again by diagonals crossing the former from the dexter side to the sinister which is the *bendy*. See *Tab. Herald. fig.* 30. the field is *paly-bendy*, topaz, and diamond.

PARTI, **PARTY**, or **PARTED**, is applied to a shield or escutcheon denoting it divided, or marked out in partitions. The *French* heralds, from whom we borrow the word, have but one kind of *parti*, the same with our *parti per pale*, which they simply call *parti* : but with us the word is applied to all sorts of partitioning; and is never used without some addition to specify the particular one intended. Thus we have *parti* or *parted per cross, per chief, per pale, per bend dexter, per bend sinister, per chevron,* &c.

The humour of our ancestors, *Colombiere* observes, turning much upon exploits and chivalry; they used to preserve their battered and hacked armour as honourable symbols of their hardy deeds; and those who had been in the hottest service, were distinguished by the most cuts and bruises that appeared on their shields. To perpetuate the memory hereof, says the author, they caused them to be painted on their shield, and thus handed down to posterity. And when heraldry grew in to an art, and officers were appointed to direct the manner of beating and blazoning; they gave names to those cuts, answerable to the nature thereof; appointing four from which all the others proceed : these are *parti* (in *English parti per pale*), *coupe* (in *English parti per fesse*), *tranche* (in *English parti per bend dexter*), and *taille* (in *English parti per bend sinister*).

PARTI *per pale*, is when the shield is divided perpendicularly into two halves, by a cut in the middle from top to bottom.

PARTI *per fesse*, is when the cut is across the middle from side to side.

PARTI *per bend dexter*, is when the cut comes from the upper corner of the shield on the right hand, and descends athwart to the lower corner.

PARTI *per bend sinister*, is when the cut, coming from the upper left corner, descends across to the lower opposite corner. From these four partitions have proceeded an infinite number of others of various and extravagant forms.

Spelman[1], in his *Aspilogia*, observes, that the present division of escutcheons was unknown in the time of *Theodosius*; were brought up in the time of *Charlemagne* or later; little used among the *English* in the days of king *Henry* II, but more frequently under *Edward* III. The erect or upright section, he observes, is called in *Latin palaris*, from its resemblance to a *palus*, or stake; and two coats are often entire on the sides, the husband's on the right, and the wife's on the left. The direct section across, being in the place of a belt, is called *baltica*.

It is said to be *parti* one from the other when the whole shield is charge with some bearing divided by the same line that parts the shield. Here it is a rule that one side be of metal, and the other of colour. Thus he bears sable, *parti* argent, a spread eagle *parti* from one to the other. When the shield is *parti* and *coupée*, it is said to be *écartelée*.

PASSANT, a term applied to an animal in a shield appearing to walk leisurely; or to the ordinary posture of terrestrial animals. Thus we say, he bears gules, two lions *passant* over one another. In most beasts, except lions, they use *tripping* instead of *passant*.

PASSION. *Cross of passion*, is a cross thus called, because in shape of that whereon our Saviour suffered, *i.e.* not crossed in the middle but nearer the top; with arms short in proportion to the length of the shaft.

PATEE, or **PATTEE**, a term in heraldry for a cross small in the centre and widening towards the extremes. See *Tab. Herald. fig.* 26. The field is sable, a cross *patee* argent by the name of *Cross*. This form of a cross is also called *formé*.

PATER-NOSTRE. A cross *pater-nostre* is a cross made of beads, as represented in *Tab. Herald. fig.* 77. This cross is to be so shadowed in drawing, as that the sphericity of the beads may appear, to distinguish them from besants, &c.

PATONCE. A *Cross Patonce* is a cross flory at the end : from which it only differs in this, that the ends instead of turning down like a flower-de-luce, are

---

[1] Sir Henry Spelman (ca. 1562 - 1641), was an English antiquary.

extended somewhat in the patee form. See *Tab. Herald. fig*. 78. He bears gules, a cross *patonce* argent, by the name of *Latimer*.

PATRIARCHAL. A *Patriarchal* cross is that where the shaft is twice crossed, the lower arms or traverses being longer, and the upper shorter. Such a cross is said to belong to *patriarchs*, as the triple cross does to the Pope.

PAVILLION, denotes a covering in form of a tent, which invests, or wraps up the armories of divers kings and sovereigns, depending only on God and their sword. The *French* heralds hold that none but sovereign monarchs may bear the pavilion entire and in all its parts.

The *pavilion* consists of two parts : the top, which is the chapeau, or coronet, and the curtain which makes the mantle. Those who are elective, or have any dependence, say the heralds, must take off the head, and retain nothing but the curtains.

The use of *pavilions* and mantles in armories is derived from the ancient lambrequins, which are sometimes found stretch out in form of coverings, and tucked back on either side.

Others will have it derived from the ancient tournaments, wherein were exposed the arms of the knights in rich tapestry work, on tents and *pavilions* which the chiefs of the quadrils planted to shelter themselves, till the time of entering the lists.

PEAN, is when the field of a coat of arms is sable and the powderings or.

PEARL, is used by such as blazon with precious stones instead of colour or metals, for argent, or white.

PELLETS, a name given to those roundels which are black.

PENDANT, a term applied to the parts hanging down from the label, to the number of three, four, five or six at most. These must be specified in blazoning when there are more than three. They resemble the drops at the bottom of the triglyphs in the Doric freeze.

PHEONS, the heads of darts, arrows, or other weapons. *Pheons* are represented in *Tab, Herald. fig*. 79. Sable, a fesse ermine between three *pheons*, by the name of *Egerton*.

PIECE, denotes an ordinary or charge. The honourable *pieces* of the shield are the chief, fess, bend, pale, bar, cross, saltier, chevron; and, in general, all those which may take up one third of the field, when alone, and in what manner soever it be.

PIERCED, PERCÉ, is when an ordinary is pierced, or struck through, showing, as it were, a hole in it. This *piercing* is to be expressed in blazon as to its shape : thus if a cross have a square hole, or perforation in the center, it is blazoned *square pierced*, which is more proper than *quarter pierced* as *Leigh* expresses it; and accordingly the *French* call it *percé au quarre*.

When the hole of perforation is round, it must be expressed *round pierced*; which *Gibbon* in *Latin* calls *perferato*, because all holes made with piercers or augers are round. If the hole set in the centre be in the shape of a lozenge, it is expressed *pierced lozenge-ways*.

All *piercings* must be the color of the field, because piercing implies showing what is under the ordinary or bearing. Though when such figures appear on the centre of a cross, &c. of another colour, the cross is not to be supposed *pierced*, but that the figure on it is a charge.

PILE, is an ordinary in form of a point inverted, or a stake sharpened; contracting from the chief and terminating in a point towards the bottom of the shield, somewhat in manner of a wedge. See *Tab. Herald. fig.* 80. It is formed probably in imitation of the *Roman* pilum, which was a tapering dart about five feet long, and sharpened at the point with steel. The *pile* is born inverted, engrailed, &c. like other ordinaries, and issues in-differently from any point on the verge of the escutcheon. He beareth a *pile* gules by the name of *Chandon*.

PLAIN, is sometimes used for the point of the shield when couped square; a part remaining under the square, of a different colour or metal from the shield. This has been sometimes used as a mark of bastardy, and called *champaigne* : for when the legitimate descendants of bastards have taken away the bar, fillet, or traverse born by their fathers, they are to cut the point of the shield, with a different colour called *plain*.

PLATE, is round flat piece of silver without any impression; but, as it were, formed ready to receive it. The term is used only by *English* heralds. In other nations they are known by the name of *bezants argent*.

POINTS, are the division of the escutcheon into several squares, sometimes to the number of 9, sometimes to 15; some whereof are of one colour or metal, others of another; called also *equipollent points*. There is also another, and that more frequent division of the escutcheon into *points*, which have several names and values, according to their several places.

There are nine principle *points* in an escutcheon as marked in *Tab. Herald. fig.* 38. A represents the *dexter chief point*. B the *middle chief point*. C the *sinister chief*. D the *honour point*. E the *fess point*. F the *nombril* or *naval point*. G the *dexter base*. I the *sinister base*. H the *precise middle base*.

As the several bearings in an escutcheon are so many types representing the commendable actions of the person they are given to; so the escutcheon itself represents the body of the man who performed them; and the *points*, or parts, signified by these letters, the principal parts of the body. Thus, A, B, C represent the head, in which the three great faculties reside; D the neck where ornaments are chiefly born; E the heart, &c. *Colombiere* makes the *points* and their situations symbolical.

POINT is also the name of an ordinary, something like the pile, rising frequently from the bottom of the escutcheon to the top, very narrow; and only taking up two thirds of the *point* of the escutcheon. When the *point* arises from the base, it is called particularly *point-in-point*.

POINT *inverted*, is when descends from the chief downwards; possessing two thirds of the chief, but diminishing as it approaches the point of the escutcheon, though without touching it.

POINT *in bend*, or *point in bar*, is when the *point* is placed transverse in the situation of a bend or bar. When it comes from the sides of the escutcheon it is also called a *point dexter* or *sinister*, according to its situation. The *point dexter* is commonly reputed an abatement due to a braggadocio. *Point-champion-ten* due for killing a prisoner after quarter demanded. *Point-in-point* a diminution belonging to a coward.

POINT is also used in heraldry for the lowest part of the escutcheon, which usually terminates in a *point*.

POINT-*Champain*. In the *French* arms the fleurs-de-lys's are two in chief, and one in *point*.

POMEIS, are green roundels, so called by the *English* heralds who express different coloured roundels by distinct names. The *French*, who content themselves to denote the different colour of the roundels, call the *pomeis*, *torteaux vert*.

POMMÉ, or **POMMETTÉ**. A *cross pommé*, or *pommetté*, called also *trophee*, is a cross with a ball or knob, like an apple, at each end.

PORTATE. A *cross portate* is a cross which does not stand upright, as crosses generally do; but lies athwart the escutcheon, in bend, as if it were carried on a man's shoulder. *Colombiere* tells us, it is by some called *porté*, that is, carried; because when our Saviour went to duffer death, he was obliged to carry his cross, which is always thus represented sloping, and inclined after this manner.

POSÉ, denotes a lion, horse, or other beast standing still with all four feet on the ground; to denote thereby that it is not in a moving posture.

QUARTER, is sometimes used for an escutcheon or coat of arms. In this sense there are sixteen *Quarters* required to prove nobility in companies or orders where none but nobles are admitted. In *Flanders* and *Germany*, we frequently see tombs which have eight, sixteen, or even thirty-two *Quarters*. The word *Quarters*, required as a proof of nobility, is derived hence, that they used anciently to put the coat of arms of the father, mother, grand-father, and grand-mother, on the four corners of the tomb of the deceased.

QUARTER is also applied to the parts, or members of the first division of a coat that is quartered, or divided into four *Quarters*; see *Tab. Herald. fig.* 45. The king of *Great Britain* in the first *Quarter* bears gules three lions passant or, &c. In the second *Quarter* he bears azure three flowers de lys, &c.

Franc **QUARTER,** is a *Quarter* single or alone; which is to possess one fourth of the field. This makes one of the honourable ordinaries of a coat.

QUARTERING, the act of dividing a coat into four or more quarters, or *Quarterings*; by parting, couping, &c. *i.e.* by perpendicular and horizontal lines. The king of *Great Britain* quarters with *France, Ireland, Brunswick,* &c.

Colombiere reckons twelve sorts of *Quarterings*, but other authors give us more, *viz.* party per pale, dividing the escutcheon from top to bottom. Party per cross, dividing it from side to side. Party of six pieces, when the escutcheon is divided into six parts or quarters. Party of ten; of twelve; of sixteen; and of thirty-two, when there are so many partitions respectively.

Others give the divisions in another manner : Party per cross – per pale – per chief – per pale inclave – per bend dexter – per bend sinister – barry bendy of eight pieces – paleways of six pieces – barry of six pieces – barry of eight pieces – bendy of six – checky – fusilly, or lozengy – paly bendy, or paly lozengy – barry bendy lozengy, or bend lozengy – gyronny – barry lozengy countercharged – waved of six pieces – barry nebule of six pieces – party per saltier – party per pale in point.

Counter **QUARTERING** *a coat*, is when the quarters are quartered over again, or subdivided each into four. There are counter-quartered coats which have twenty or twenty-five quarters.

QUARTERING is also applied to the partitions or compartments themselves, that is, the several coats born on an escutcheon, or the several divisions made in it, when the arms of several families are to be placed on the same shield, on account of intermarriages, or the like.

Colombiere observes, that thirty-two is the greatest number used in France, but that the *English* and *German* sometimes extend to forty; as a testimony to the truth whereof, he says, he saw the escutcheon of the earl of *Leicester*, ambassador extraordinary in *France* in the year 1639, divided into the number of forty; and some he affirms, do go on to sixty four several coats. But a multitude of quarters makes a confusion; and accordingly all the writers of armory cry out against it as an abuse.

The first instance of *Quartering* whereof we have any account, is said to be in the arms of *Renatus*, king of *Sicily*, &c. in the year 1435, who quartered the arms of *Sicily, Arragon, Jerusalem,* &c.

William Wickley, observes that such *Quarterings* are much properer for a pedigree to be locked up in a chest, and occasionally produced for the clearing or ascertaining of alliances of families, or titles to lands, &c. than to be born as a cognizance.

In blazoning, when the *Quartering* is performed per cross, the two quarters atop are numbered the first and second; and those at the bottom the third and fourth; beginning to tell on the right side. When the *Quartering* is by a saltier, &c. the chief and point are the first and second quarter, the right side the third, the left the fourth.

QUARTERLY. A person is said to bear *Quarterly*, when he bears arms quartered. The king of *Great Britain* bears *Quarterly* four; in the first quarter gules, &c. *Great Britain* : in the second azure, &c. *Ireland*, &c.

QUEUE, the tail of a beast. If a lion have a forked tail, he is blazoned *double-queued*.

ℜ

RACOURCY, signifies the same as *coupy*, that is, cut off, or shortened; and denotes a cross or other ordinary when it does not extend to the edges of the escutcheon, as they do when absolutely named, without such distinction.

RAGULED, or **RAGGED**, is applied to an ordinary, *e.gr.* a cross, whose outlines are jagged or knotted. See *Tab. Herald. fig.* 58. He beareth sable, a cross *raguled*, or, by the name of *Sloway*. The bearing is very ancient : *Julius Caesar* gave for his badge a boar's head on a *ragged* staff.

RAMPANT, is applied to a lion, bear, leopard, or other beast, in a posture of climbing, or standing upright on his hind-legs, and rearing up his fore-feet; shewing only half his face, as one eye and one ear. The term is *French* and signifies literally *creeping.*

It is different from *salient*, which denotes a posture less erect, or somewhat stooping forwards, as if making a sally. This posture is to be specified in blazoning in all animals, except in the lion and griffon; it being their natural situation.

REGARDANT, is understood of a lion, or other beast of prey, borne in a posture of looking behind him, with his face towards his tail. Others apply it to a beast which only shews its head, and some part of the neck, as moving from out of some division of the coat into another. He bears azure, three bends, or, in a chief argent, charged with a lion *regardant* gules.

REMPLY, something filled up. The term is chiefly used to denote that the chief is quite filled up with a square piece of another colour, leaving only a bordure of the proper colour of the chief about the said piece.

RENVERSE, *inverse*, is when any thing is set with the head downwards, or contrary to its natural way of being. Thus a chevron *renverse* is a chevron with the point downwards. The same term they also use when a beast is laid down on its back.

REVERSED, a thing turned backwards or upside-down.

ROMPEE, or **ROMPU**, is applied to ordinaries that are represented as broken; and to chevrons whose upper point is cut off. As in *Tab. Herald. fig.*

83. He beareth a chevron *rompee*, between three mullets, argent, by the name of *Sault*.

RUBY, denotes the red colour wherewith the arms of noblemen are blazoned; being the same which in the arms of others not noble is called *gules*.

RUNDELS, or **ROUNDELS**, the same as balls or pellets.

SABLE, the black colour in the arms of gentlemen. In those of nobility it is called *Diamond*; and in the coats of foreign princes, *Saturn*. It is expressed in engraving by perpendicular and horizontal hatches drawn a-cross each other – as represented in *Tab. Herald. fig.* 27. The name is borrowed from the little animal called *Sable*, which is of a black colour.

SALIENT, SALIANT, or **SALLIANT**, is applied to a lion, or other beast, when its fore-legs are raised in a leaping posture. A lion *Saliant* is that which is erected bend-ways : standing so as that his right fore-foot is in the dexter chief point, and his hinder left foot, in the sinister base point of the escutcheon. By which it is distinguished from rampant.

SALTIER, SALTEER, or **SALTIRE**, an ordinary in form of a St. *Andrew's* cross; anciently called the cross of *Burgundy*. The *Saltier* may be said to be composed of a bend dexter and sinister, crossing each other in the centre of the escutcheon. See *Tab. Herald. fig.* 35. See also the article *Bend*.

Its ordinary breadth, when alone, is one third of the escutcheon. It is sometimes bore alaisé, and sometimes in number, placed in different parts of the field : sometimes charged, sometimes countercharged with the field, accompanied, raguled, engrailed, indented, quarterly-quartered, &c.

The *Saltier* was anciently a piece of the knight's harness; being fastened to the saddle, and serving him for a stirrup to mount upon; and it was hence it had its name *Saltier*, by the *French Sautoir*, from *Sauter*, to leap. It was made of silk cord, or some other kind of cord, covered with some rich stuff.

Others will have it, that the original *Saltier* was a kind of palisade, serving to fence parks, woods, &c. where wild beasts were enclosed. Though *Spelman* says, it was an instrument for the taking them, thus called *Quod sit in usu in Saltu*. Lastly, others assure us, that *Saltier* was anciently the figure of an engine, which being full of pins, was used in the scaling of the walls of a besieged place : whence its origin from *Sauter*, as helped the soldiers to leap over the walls.

SANGUINE, the colour usually called *Murry*; being made of red lake, tinged with a little *Spanish* brown. It is represented in engraving by transverse hatches like purpure; and is mostly used in the coats of the knights of the Bath. When borne by nobles it is mostly called *Sardonyx*; and the coats of sovereign princes, *Dragon's Tail*.

SATURN, denotes the black colour in the coats of arms of sovereign princes; answering to diamond in the coats of noblemen; and sable in those of gentlemen.

SCARP, is a term in heraldry, probably derived from the *French escharpe*, signifying the scarf, which military commanders wear for ornament. It is borne something like a battoon sinister, but is broader and continued out to the edges of the field; whereas the battoon is cut off at each end. He beareth argent, a *scarp* azure.

SEGREANT, is the heralds word for a griffon, when drawn in a leaping posture, and displaying his wings as if ready to fly.

SEJANT, is a term used in heraldry, when a lion, or other beast, is drawn in an escutcheon, sitting like a cat, with his fore-feet straight.

SHIELD, denotes the escutcheon or field whereon the bearings of an armory are placed.

SINISTER. The *sinister* side of an escutcheon is the left-hand side.

SINISTER *side of the base*, is the left-hand part of the base.

SINISTER *bend*. See the article *Bend*.

SINOPLE, or **SENOPLE**, denotes *vert*, or the green colour in armories. Thus called by the ancient heralds; though *Pliny* and *Isidore*[1], *color prasinus*[2], or *sinople*, mean a brownish red, such as that of our ruddle. F.

---

[1] Saint Isidore of Seville (ca. 560 – 636), was the Archbishop of Seville.
[2] Prasinus is the same as leek green.

Menestrier[1] derives the word from the *Greek prasina hoopla*, green armories; by corruptedly retrenching the first syllable *pra*; which is no new thing among oriental words; witness *Salonica* for *Thessalonica*. *Sinople* is supposed to signify love, youth, beauty, rejoicing, and liberty; whence it is, that letters of grace, abolition, legitimation, &c. are used to be sealed with green wax.

STAFF. See the article *Batoon*.

STAR, denotes a charge frequently borne on the shield, and honourable ordinaries, in the figure of a *star*. It usually consists of five rays or spokes. When it has six or eight, as among the *Germans* and *Italians*, particular mention must be made thereof in blazoning. It differs from the *mullet*, or spur-rowel, in that it is not pierced as the last is.

SUPPORTED, a term applied to the upper quarters of a shield, when divided into several quarters; these seeming, as it were, *supported* or sustained by those below. The chief is also said to be *supported* when it is of two colours, and the upper colour takes up two thirds of it : in this case it is *supported* by the colour underneath.

SUPPORTING, figures in an atchievement, placed by the side of the shield, and seeming to *support*, or hold up the same. *Supporters* are chiefly figures of beasts; figures of human creatures used for the like purpose are more properly called *tenants*. Some make another difference between *tenant* and *supporter* : when the shield is bore by a single animal, it is called *tenant*; when by two, they are called *supporters*.

The figures of things inanimate sometimes placed on the sides of escutcheons but not touching, or seeming to bear them; though sometimes called *supporters*, are more properly called *cotises*.

The *supporters* of the *English* arms are the lion and an unicorn; some of the former kings had a leopard and an unicorn; others griffons; others eagles. The *supporters* of the *French* arms are angels; which are said to have been first introduced by *Philip* VI, his device being an angel overthrowing a dragon : the dragon at that time being the device of king of *England*. Those of the Prince of *Monaco* are *Augustine* monks : those of the family of the *Ursini*, bears, in allusion to their names.

In *England*, none below the degree of banneret are allowed *supporters*, which are those restrained to the high nobility. The *Germans* permit none but princes and noblemen of rank to bear them. Among the *French* the use is more promiscuous.

---

[1] Claude-François Ménestrier (1631 – 1705), was a French Jesuit, heraldist and attendant of the royal court.

SURMOUNTED, is when one figure is laid over another. As the pile *surmounted* of a chevron, in *Tab. Herald. fig.* 48.

𝕿

TABLE. Coats, or escutcheons, containing nothing but the mere colour of the field, and not charged any bearing, figure, moveable, &c. are called *Tables d'Attente*, *Tables of Expectation*, or *Tabulae Rasae*.

TAIL, is particularly used for the *tail* of a hart; those of several other creatures having peculiar and distinct names. As, that of a buck, roe, or any other deer, is called the *Single*; of a boar, the *Wreath*; of a fox, the *Bush*; of a wolf, the *Stern*; and of a hare and cony, the *Scut*.

TAILLÉ, or **TAILEE**. See *Tranché*.

TAU, or **TAW**, an ordinary in figure of a T, supposed to represent St. *Andrew's* cross, or a cross potence, with the top part cut off. It is thus called from the name of the *Greek* T, *tau*.

TENANT, or **TENON**, is used for something that sustains, or holds up the shield, or armory; and is generally synonymous with *supporter*.

The difference which some authors make between the two is, that *tenants* are in single, and supporters double, one placed on each side of the shield. But the proper distinction seems to consist in this, that *tenants* are human figures, and supporters figures of beasts.

There are various forms of *tenants*, as well as supporters, *viz.* angels, maids, religious, savages, *Moors*, &c.

The first *tenants*, F. *Menestrier* observes, where trunks or branches of trees; to which the escutcheons were fastened by straps and buckles. Afterwards, the knights were represented as holding their own escutcheons, which were either hung to their neck, or else they leaned on them.

The origins of *tenants* and supporters is referred to the ancient tournaments, whereas the cavaliers had their arms born by servants disguised like savages, *Moors*, fabulous deities, bears, lions, &c.

TENNE, TENNY, or **TAWNY**, a bright colour made of red and yellow mixed; and sometimes also called *brusk*, and expressed in engraving by thwart or diagonal strokes or hatches, beginning from the sinister chief, like purpure, and marked with the letter T. In the coats of all below the degree of nobles, it is called *tenny*; but in those of nobles, it is called *hyacinth*; and in prince's coats, the *dragon's head*.

TIERCED, TIERCÉ, denotes the shield to be divided by any of the partition lines, party, coupy, tranchy, or tailly, into three equal parts, of different colours or metals. If the chief and base be of the same colour when divided by a fesse, they blazon it by expressing the colour and mentioning the fesse; otherwise, they say it is *tierce in fesse*, and mention each of the colours; or *tiercé in pale*, if so divided in pale.

TIMBER, or **TIMMER**, denotes the crest of an armoury, or whatever is placed a-top of the escutcheon to distinguish the degree of nobility, either ecclesiastical or secular. Such is the papal tiara, cardinal's hat, cross, mitre, coronet, mortier, and particularly the casks of helmets, which the ancients called more especially *timbres*, from their resembling a kind of bell without a clapper, which the *French* call *timbre*, or because they resounded like those *timbres* when struck. This is the opinion of *Loiseau*, who derives the word from the *Latin tintinnabulum*.

TIMBERS *of ermines*, denote the ranks or rows of ermine in noblemen's coats.

TOISON *d'Or*, a term in heraldry for a golden fleece which is sometimes borne in a coat of arms.

TORQUE, a round roll of cloth twisted and stuffed; such is the bandage frequently seen in armories, about the heads of *Moors*, savages, &c. It is always of the two principal colours of the coat, The *torque* is the least honourable of all the enrichments wore on the helmet by way of crest.

TRANCHÉ, or **TRENCHÉ**, is used by the *French* armorists, to express that manner of partition called among us, *party per bend dexter*. An escutcheon is said to be *tranché*, cut, when it is divided in two diagonally, the division coming from the dexter angle of the chief to the sinister angle of the point : when it is divided contrary-wise, it is said to be *taillé*, or *party per bend sinister*.

TRIANGLE, the diminutive of a fesse, commonly called a *bar*.

TRESSURE, a diminutive of an orle, usually supposed to be half the breadth thereof. It is usually born flory, and counter-flory; and sometimes double, as in *Tab. Herald. fig.* 85. and sometimes triple.

TRIPPING, denotes the quick motion of all sorts of deer, and other sorts of creatures, represented with one foot up, as it were on a trot. In speaking of lions, they say *passant*, instead of *tripping*.

𝖁

VAIR, a kind of fur, or doubling, consisting of divers little pieces, argent and azure, resembling a *Dutch* U, or bell-glass. *Vairs* have the point azure opposite to their point argent, and based argent to the azure. When there are only two or three *vairs*, the ancient heralds call it *great vair*; when three or more *small vair*.

Vair is intended to represent a kind of skin, used anciently by the kings of *France*, in lieu of a fur, and wherewith the gowns of the presidents a mortier, the counselors of the court, the heralds coats, &c. were lined till the fifteenth century.

It was properly the skin of a kind of squirrel, called also in *French vair*, and in *Latin scriveus*; which was white underneath and a dove-colour a-top. It is describe by *Aldrovandus*[1], under the name of *scriveo* varia, and is the same, according to *Gesner*[2], with the *mus ponticus* of *Aristotle* and *Pliny*; which the *Latins* call varus, or varius, from the variety of its colour. Its two skins joined together make the *vairs* in armories; being naturally white and azure.

Vair, *Colombiere* observes, is the second sort of fur, anciently used as the lining of the garments of great men, consisting of little pieces, sewed by the farriers on white skins : and because these pieces were usually blue, those who first settled the rules of heraldry, decreed, that this fur, in its natural blazon, should always be argent and azure. So if it be absolutely said, such a family bears *vair*; it is supposed to be argent and azure.

---

[1] Probably Ulisse Aldrovandi (1522 – 1605), who was an Italian naturalist.
[2] Probably Conrad, or Konrad, Gesner (1516 – 1565), who was a Swiss naturalist and bibliographer.

Regularly, there must be but four rows or ranks of *vair* in the shield; if there be either more or less, the number must be specified. The smallest number, being three rows is called *beffroy de vair*; and the most, being five or six, is called *menu* or *small vair*.

The *beffroy* is also known by the first figure on the dexter-side of the escutcheon, being always of metal, and in form of a belt; whereas that of mere *vair* is in shape of a glass.

VAIRY, **VAIRÉ**, **VERRY**, or **VARRY**, is applied to a coat, or the bearings of a coat, when charged, or chequered with *vair*. When the colours are argent and azure, or white and blue, it is very proper; if it be otherwise, the colours are to be expressly named; *vairy* of such a colour or metal. He bears *vairy* or, and vert : this is particularly called *vair composed*.

The bearings are likewise said to be *vairy* when they are charge with *vairs*. When chiefs, crosses, pales, &c. happen to be *vairy*, the number of ranks are to be specified.

Vairy gowns are observed, by *Julius Pollux*[1], to have been the habit of the ancient *Gauls*, as ermins were of the *Armenians*.

VAIRY *Cuppy*, or **VAIRY** *Tassy*, or *Potent Counter-potent*, is a bearing in heraldry, composed of pieces representing the tops of crutches. See *Tab. Herald. fig.* 87. In blazon, the colours must be expressed, as azure, argent, &c.

VERDOY, is applied to a bordure of a coat of arms, charged with any kinds or parts of flowers, fruits, seeds, plants, &c.

VERT, the term for a green colour. It is called *vert* in the blazon of the coats of all under the degree of nobles; but in coats of nobles it is called *emerald*; and in those of kings, *Venus*. In engraving it is expressed by diagonals, or lines drawn athwart, from right to left, from the dexter chief corner, to the sinister base. See *Tab. Herald. fig.* 48. In lieu of *vert*, the *French* heralds use sinople, or synople.

VOIDED, **VUIDÉ**, is understood of an ordinary whose inner or middle part is cut out; leaving nothing but its edges to shew its form; so that the field appears through it. Hence, it is needless to express the colour or metal of the *voided* part; because it must, of course, be that of the field.

The Cross **VOIDED**, differ from the cross *fimbriated*, in that this latter does not shew the field through it, as the other does. And the same obtains in other ordinaries.

---

[1] Julius Pollux (circa 2nd century AD), was a Greek grammarian, sophist, scholar and rhetorician.

VOIDER, one of the ordinaries, whose figure is much like that of the flasque or flanch; only that it doth not bend so much. See *Tab. Herald. fig.* 89. See also the article *Flanch.* This armoury, they say, is properly the reward of a gentlewoman that has well served her prince. It is always borne by pairs.

VOL, among heralds, signifies the two wings of a fowl joined together borne in armoury; as being the whole that makes the flight. Accordingly, a *demi-vol* is a single wing.

VOLANT, is when a bird in a coat of arms is drawn flying, or having its wings spread out.

U

UPRIGHT, is used in respect of shell-fishes, as crevices, &c. when standing erect in a coat. Inasmuch as they want fins, they cannot, according to *Guillim*, be properly said to be *hauriant*[1]; that being a term appropriated to scaly fishes.

URDÉ, or **URDÉE**. A *cross urdé* seems to be the same with what we otherwise call clechée.

---

[1] In heraldry, a fish or water animal, being in pale with the head up as if rising for air.

WAVED, or **WAVY**, a term in heraldry, when a bordure, or any ordinary in a coat of arms, has its outlines indented, in manner of the rising and falling of *waves*. This is also called *undy*, *undé*, or *ondé*.

WINGS, are borne sometimes single, sometimes in pairs, in which case they are called *conjoined*; when the points are downwards they are said to be *inverted*; when up, *elevated*. See *Vol*.

WINGED, is applied to a bird when its wings are of a different colour or metal from the body.

WREATH, a roll of fine linen, or silk, (like that of a Turkish turban) consisting of the colours borne in the escutcheon, in an atcheivement, between the helmet and the crest, and immediately supporting the crest.

HERALDRY.

ILLERION Fig. 1.   ANNULET Fig. 2.   AZURE Fig. 3.   BARRY-BENDY Fig. 4.   BARRY-PILY Fig. 5.

BASTON Fig. 6.   BEND Fig. 7.   BEVILE Fig. 8.   BILLET Fig. 9.   BORDURE Fig. 10.

BOTTONY Fig. 11.   CANTON Fig. 12.   CARBUNCLE Fig. 13.   CHAPPE Fig. 14.   CHECKY Fig. 15.

CHEVRON Fig. 16.   BRACED Fig. 17.   DIAPRE Fig. 18.   COMPONE Fig. 19.   FER DE FOURCHETTE Fig. 20.

FER DE MOULIN Fig. 21.   FESSE Fig. 22.   FILE Fig. 23.   FITCHEE Fig. 24.   FLANCH Fig. 25.

FLORY Fig. 26.   SABLE Fig. 27.   NAISSANT Fig. 28.   MANTLING Fig. 29.   PALY BENDY Fig. 30.

PALISSE Fig. 31.   NEBULE Fig. 32.   FOURCHEE Fig. 33.   MASCLE Fig. 34.   SALTIER Fig. 35.

CLARION Fig. 36.   CLECHE Fig. 37.   ESCUTCHEON POINTS Fig. 38.   FRET Fig. 39.   MAUNCH Fig. 40.

CHIEF Fig. 41.   FUSIL Fig. 42.   COEUR Fig. 43.   SCARPE Fig. 44.   QUARTER Fig. 45.

A B C
D
E F
G H I

HERALDRY *Tab.II.*

BENDY   POTENT   RAGULED   PALE   COUNTER-CHANGED
Fig.46   Fig.47   Fig.48   Fig.49   Fig.50

COUNTER-COMPOSED   CRAMPONEE   HAURIANT   CROSSELET   PALL
Fig.51   Fig.52   Fig.53   Fig.54   Fig.55

GULES   ENGRAILED   ENDORSE   EMBATTLED   ERMINE
Fig.56   Fig.57   Fig.58   Fig.59   Fig.60

COTICE   ERMINEE   ERMINES   ESCUTCHEON of Pretence   GIRONEE
Fig.61   Fig.62   Fig.63   Fig.64   Fig.65

  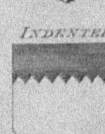 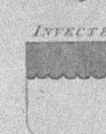 

GORE   GUSSET   INDENTED   INVECTED   LOZENGE
Fig.66   Fig.67   Fig.68   Fig.69   Fig.70

  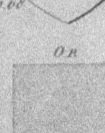  

MARTLET   MULLET   OR   ORLE   PATEE
Fig.71   Fig.72   Fig.73   Fig.74   Fig.75

    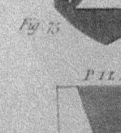

PATER-NOSTER   PATONCE   PEAN   PHEON   PILE
Fig.76   Fig.77   Fig.78   Fig.79   Fig.80

    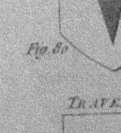

PURPURE   RIBBAN   ROMPEE   SURMOUNTED   TRAVERSE
Fig.81   Fig.82   Fig.83   Fig.84   Fig.85

TRESSURE   VAIRE   VAIRY CUPPY   VERT   VOIDER
Fig.86   Fig.87   Fig.88   Fig.89   Fig.90

HERALDRY Tab.III.

HELMET

Fig.91. Fig.92. Fig.93. Fig.94. Fig.95. Nº Fig.95.

CHAPEAU.

Esquire. Baronets & Knights. Marques Earls &c. Dukes. Kings.

Fig.96. CROWN Fig.97. Fig.98. Fig.99.

Oval. Naval. Castrensis. Mural.

Fig.100. Fig.101. Fig.102. Fig.103.

Civic. Triumphal. Obsidionalis. Radial.

Fig.104. Fig.105. Fig.106. Fig.107.

Papal. Imperial. English. French.

Fig.108. Fig.109. Fig.110. Fig.111.

Spanish. Turkish. Electoral. Prince of Wales.

Fig.112. Fig.113. Fig.114. Fig.115.

Plume of Feathers. Younger Sons &c. Nephews. Princesses.

Fig.116. Fig.117. Fig.118. Fig.119.

Dukes. Marquis. Earls. Viscount.

Fig.120. Fig.121. CROSIER. Fig.122.

Baron. MITRE.

HERALDRY *Tab IV*

HATCHMENT

Fig. 123

Fig. 124

Fig. 125

Fig. 126

Fig. 127

Fig. 128

Fig. 129

Fig. 130

WREATH *Fig. 131*

MILITARY ART

𝔄

ADVANCE-FOSSE, or *Ditch*, in fortification, denotes a ditch of water round the esplanade, or glacis of the place; to prevent its being surprised by the besiegers. See *Fosse* and *Glacis*.

ADVANCE-GUARD, or *Van-Guard*, is the first line or division of army ranged, or marching in battle-array; or that part which is next the enemy, or which marches first towards them. The whole body of an army is divided into *Advance-guard*, arrear-guard, and main body. The word is also sometimes applied to a small body of horse, *viz.* 15 or 20, commanded by a lieutenant, beyond, and in sight of, the main guard.

ALARM-POST, is the ground appointed to each regiment, by the quarter-master-general, for them to march to in case of an alarm. In a garrison, the alarm-post is a place where every regiment is ordered to draw up on ordinary occasions.

AMBUSCADE, AMBUSHE, AMBUSHMENT, a body of men who lie hid in a wood, &c. to rush out upon, or inclose and enemy unawares. Or the place wherein such a corps hide themselves.

ANTESTATURE, in fortification, a small retrenchment, made of pallisadoes, or sacks of earth, made up in haste, to dispute with the enemy the remainder of a piece of ground, part whereof hath been already gained. See *Retrenchment*.

APPROACHES, in fortification, the several works made by the besiegers for advancing or getting nearer to a fortress, or place besieged. Such are trenches, mines, saps, lodgments, batteries, galleries, epaulments.

APPROACHES, or *Lines of Approach*, are particularly used for trenches dug in the ground, and the earth thrown up on the side next the place besieged; under shelter or defence whereof the besiegers may approach, without loss, to the parapet of the covered way, and plant guns, &c. wherewith to cannonade the place. The lines of *approach* are to be connected by parallels or lines of communication. The besieged frequently make *counter-approaches* to interrupt and defeat the enemies *approaches*.

ARRAIGNEE, in fortification, sometimes denotes a branch, return, or gallery of a mine.

ARBELET, a weapon, vulgarly called a crossbow. The word is derived from *arbalista*, *i.e. arcubullista*, a bow with a sling. The *arbelet* consists of a steel bow, set in a shaft of wood, furnished with a string and a trigger; and is bent with a piece of iron fitted. for that purpose. It serves to throw bullets, large arrows, darts, &c. The ancients had large machines to throw arrows withal, called *arbelets*, or *ballistae*. See *Balista*.

ARCHERS, a kind of militia or soldiery armed with bows and arrows. *Archers* were much in use in former times; but are not laid aside, excepting in *Turkey*, and some of the eastern countries; where there are companies of arches still on foot on their armies; with which they did terrible execution at the battle of *Lepanto*.

The name *archer*, however, is still retained even where the thing is lost : thus, in *France*, the officers who attend lieutenants de police, and provosts, to make captures, seizures, arrests, &c. are called *archers*; though their arms be only halberds or carabines. In this sense they say, the *archers* of the *grand prevot de l'hotel*; of the *prevot de marchands*; the city *archers*; the *archers du guet*, or of the watch, &c. Small parties of *archers*, called also *marechaussée*, are continually patrolling on the great roads, to secure them against robbers. The *Diligences* of *Lyon* are always escorted by a party of *archers*.

To the diligence of these *archers* or marshals men, it is owing, that persons now travel in all parts of *France* in the utmost security; there being fewer robberies on the highway in the whole kingdom in a year, than about *London* in a week. They also have their *archers des pauvres*, or *archers* of the poor; whose office it is to seize such beggars as they find in the streets, and carry them to the hospitals.

The word is formed from the Latin *arcus*; whence *arcuarius*, even *arquis*, and *arquites*, as they are also denominated in the corrupt state of that tongue.

ARMOR, ARMOUR, a defensive habit, wherewith to cover and secure the body from the attacks of the enemy. In ancient statutes this is frequently called *harness*. Such are the buckler[1], cuirasse[2], helmet, gauntlet, &c.

---

[1] A small round shield about one to one and half foot in diameter.
[2] A breastplate reaching from the neck to the waist

A compleat *armor* anciently consisted of a casque or helm, a gorget, cuirasses, gauntlets, tasses[1], brassets[2], cuisses[3], and covers for the legs, to which the spurs were attached. This they called *armor cap-a-pe*; and was the wear of the cavaliers and men at arms.

The infantry had only part of it, *viz.* a pot or head-piece, a cuirasse, and tasses; but all light. Lastly, the horses themselves had their armor, wherewith to cover the head and neck.

Of all this furniture of war, scarce any thing is now retained except the cuirasse : the gorget or neck-piece, worn by officers, being at present only a badge of honour, and of no defence. The gallantry of going to the battle naked, without any defensive armor, prevailed so far, that the *French*, during the reign of *Louis* XIV, were obliged to be continually issuing ordinances to restrain it; in consequence of which, the general officers, and those of the cavalry, were obliged to resume the cuirasse, which yet has been but ill observed.

ARMORY, **ARMOUR**, a store-house of arms, or a place where military habiliments are kept to be ready for use. There are *armories* in the tower, and all arsenals, citadels, castles, etc.

ARMY, a large body of soldiers, consisting of horse and foot, under the command of a general, with several ranks of subordinate officers under him. This is to be understood of a land *army*. A naval or sea *army* is a number of ships of war, equipped and manned with sailors and marines, under the command of an admiral, with other inferior officers under him.

We say, an *army* ranged in order of battle. The march of any *army*, The retreat of an *army*. The review of an *army*. Besiegers are obliged to have an *army* of observation, to prevent relief being brought into the place, or the siege being raised. *Vid. Savin, Nouv. Ecol. Milit*[4]. p. 355, seq.

An *army* consists of squadrons and battalions, and is usually divided into three corps, which are ranged in three lines. The first line is called the vanguard; the second, the main body; and the third, the rear guard or body of reserve. The middle of each line is possessed by foot; the cavalry forms the wings on the right and left of each line; and sometimes they also place squadrons of horse in the intervals between the battalions.

When the *army* is ranged in order of battle, there are five feet distance between every two horses, and three between the foot. But in the shock the file contracts, and its front lessens to almost one half.

In each line the battalions are distant from each other about 180 foot, a distance about equal to the extent of their front; and the same holds of the

---

[1] Pieces of armour covering the thighs consisting if small overlapping metal plates.
[2] Brassarts are pieces of plate armour covering the arms.
[3] Refers to a piece of armour covering the thigh.
[4] Nouvelle école militaire, ou la Fortification moderne, &c. by Pierre Samuel Desprez De Saint Savin (1735)

squadrons, which are about 300 foot distant, the extent of their own front. These intervals are left for the squadrons and battalions of the second line to range themselves against the intervals of the first line; and those of third line against those of the second; that both the one and the other may march more readily through these spaces to the enemy.

There are usually 300 foot left between the first line and the second, and 600 between the second line and the third; that there may be room to rally when the squadrons and battalions are broke. *Savin. Nouv. Ecol. Milit.*, p. 266.

Long experience has shown that in *Europe* a prince with a million of subjects cannot keep an *army* of above ten thousand men without ruining himself. It was otherwise in the ancient republics : the proportion of soldiers to the rest of the people, which is now about one to one hundred, might then be as about one to eight. The reason seems owing to that equal partition of lands, which the ancient founders of commonwealths made among their subjects so that every man had a considerable property to defend. Whereas among us, the lands and riches of a nation being share among a few, the rest have no way of subsisting but by way of trades, arts, and the like : and have neither any free property to defend, nor means to enable them to go to war in defence of it, without starving their families. A large part of our people are either artisans or servants, so only minister to the luxury and effeminacy of the great.

While the quality of lands subsisted, *Rome*, though only a little state, being refused the succours the *Latins* were obliged to furnish after the taking of the city in the consulate of *Camillus*, presently raised ten legions within their own walls : which was more, *Livy* assures us, than they were able to do in his time, though masters of the greatest part of the world. A full proof, adds the historian, we are not grown stronger; and that what swells our city is only luxury, and the means and effects of it. *Vid. Liv. Dec.* I. l. 7. *Consid. Sur le Caus. de la Grand. de Rom.* c. 3. p. 24.

Our *armies* anciently were a sort of militia compose chiefly of the vassals and tenants of the lord. When each company had served the number of days or months enjoined by their tenure, or the customs of the sees they held, they returned home.

The *armies* of the empire consist of divers bodies of troops, furnished by the several circles.

The gross of the *French* armies under the *Merovingian* race consisted of infantry. Under *Pepin* and *Charlemaign*, the armies consisted almost equally of cavalry and foot : but since the declension of the *Carlovingian* line, the sees being become hereditary, the national armies, says *le Gendre*, are chiefly cavalry.

ARQUEBUSS, or **HARQUEBUSS**, a large hand-gun, something bigger than our musket; and called by some a *caliever*. The word is derived from the *Italian arcobusio*, or *arcoabuso*, formed of *arco*, a bow, and *busio*, a hole;

because of the touch-hole of an *arquebuss*, which succeeds to the use of the bow among the ancients.

ARQUEBUSS *a Croc*, is a sort of small fort-arm, which carries a ball of about three half ounces; now only used in old *Castille*, and some garrisons of the *French*.

ARSENAL, a royal or public magazine, or place appointed for the making and keeping of arms necessary either for defense or assault. The *arsenal* of *Venice* is where the galleys are build and laid up. The *arsenal* of *Paris* is that where the cannon or great guns are cast. There are also *arsenals*, or store-houses, appropriate to naval furniture and equipments. At *Marseilles* is the arsenal for the gallies; at *Toulon, Rochfort, Brest*, for the men of war.

The word, according to some, is derived from *arx, arcis*, fortress; by others from *ars*, engine; this being the place where the engines of war were preserved. Some will have it compounded of *arx* and *senatus*, as being the defence of the senate; others fetch from the *Italian arsenale*, or from the modern *Greek arsenalis*; but the most probable opinion is, that is derived from *darsenaa*, which, in the *Arabic*, signifies an *arsenal*.

ARTILLERY, the heavy equipage of war; comprehending all sorts *debellatura* of great fire-arms; as cannons, mortars, bombs, petards, musquets, carbines, &c. In this sense the word *artillery* coincides with what we call *ordnance*. There was no attacking such a place for want of *artillery*.

The *Persians* we are told, in the embassy of *Figueroa*, would never, in 1518, have either *artillery* or infantry in their armies, by reason they hinder their charging, and retiring with so much nimbleness; wherein their chief military address and glory lay.

The term *artillery* is sometimes also applied to the ancient instruments of war, as the catapultae, battering rams, &c.

Park of **ARTILLERY**, is that place in a camp set apart for the *artillery* or large fire-arms.

Traile or Train of **ARTILLERY**, is a set or certain number of pieces of ordnance, mounted on carriages, with all their furniture fit for marching. To it frequently belong mortar-pieces, with bombs, carcasses, &c. under the direction of the master of the *artillery*. There are trains of *artillery* in most of the king's magazines as in the Tower, *Portsmouth, Plymouth, Windsor*, &c.

ARTILLERY *Company*, is a band of infantry, consisting of 600 men, making part of the militia or city-guard of *London*.

ARTILLERY is also used for what we otherwise call pyrotechnia, or the art of fire-works, with the instruments and apparatus belonging to them.

The writers upon artillery are *Casimir Semionowitz*, *Buchnerus*, *Brownius*, *Mieth*, and *S. Remy* in his *Memoirs d'Artillerie*, which contains an accurate description of all the machines and instruments of war now in use, with every thing that relates thereto.

ASSAULT, in the art of war, an attack made upon a camp, fortress, or posts, in order to carry or become master thereof. An *assault* is properly a general furious attack, whereby the assailants do not screen themselves by any works. We say, to give an *assault*, to be commanded to an *assault*, to stand an *assault*, to repulse an *assault*, to carry an *assault*, &c. While an *assault* lasts, and both parties are mixed, the fire of the batteries ceases; there is no use of cannon on either side; for they are afraid of destroying their own men thereby.

A governour is obliged to sustain three *assaults* ere he give up the place. It is very difficult saving a town from pillage that is carried by *assault*. The *enfants perdu* march first to the *assault*.

Few places of late years stand *assaults*; M. *de Feuquiere* [1]finds but three in his time. The first was *Neuhasel*, in 1683, commanded by the *Turkish* bashaw: it was take as most others must be, because the column of infantry that marched to the breach consisted of more ranks than that of the infantry which defended it. The second was *Buda*, the bashaw of which was killed in the attack. He had some flanking works remaining, whose fires had not been entirely ruined by the artillery of the besiegers. The third was the castle of *Namur*, defended by M. *de Boufflers*, which was not carried, by reason the column of infantry which attacked the breach, marched from too far off unsheltered. Add, that it is almost impossible to carry a place by storm, when the breach may be defended by the fires of works not yet destroyed. In reality, it should be defended by no other fires, but those which are opposed to it in front, or from the breach itself.

Such obstinacy in defending places to the last extremity is no longer found, except among the *Turks*; among whom it is a point of religion not to surrender to the Christians by capitulation, any place where they have once had a mosque. Though of late they have sometimes departed from this maxim.

ASSEMBLY, is used in the military art, for the second beat of the drum, being that before the march. On hearing this, the soldiers strike their tents, roll them up, then stand to their arms. The third beating is called the *march*, as the first is called the *general*.

---

[1] Antoine de Pas de Feuquières (1648 – 1711), was a French soldier and served under king Louis XIV

ATTACK, in the military art, is an attempt or engagement to force a post, a body of troops, or the like. We say to begin, to make, to sustain an *attack*, &c. Several authors have wrote of the art of attacking and defending.

ATTACK *of a siege*, is an effort made by the besiegers with trenches, mines, galleries, &c. to make themselves masters of a fortress, in attacking one of its sides. It is a rule always to attack on the weakest side; unless there be superior reasons for the contrary – as was the case at the siege of *Lisle* : the part where prince *Eugene* made his attack was the strongest in the whole place. *Savin. Nouv, Ecol. Milit.* p. 338. seq.

False **ATTACK**, is that which is not so vigorously prosecuted, serving only to make a diversion among the besieged, and to oblige them to divide their forces, that the true *attack* may be carried on with greater success.

To **ATTACK** *in flank*, is to attack both side of the bastion.

𝕭

BACULE, in fortification, a kind of portcullis or gate, made like a pit-fall with a counter-poise, and supported by two great stakes. It is usually made before the *corps du gard*, advancing near the gate.

BALLISTA, a military engine in use among the ancients, somewhat like our cross-bow, though much bigger and more forcible; used in the besieging of cities, to throw in stones, or sometimes darts and javelins.

The word is also frequently written without its etymon, *ballista*, sometimes *balistra*. It is formed from the *Greek* βαλλειν, *jacere*, being chiefly used in casting of darts, and arrows, in which it differed from the *catapulta*, which was used only for casting stones; in other respects they were alike, and were each bent in the same manner.

Marcellinus[1] describes the *ballista* thus; a round iron cylinder is fastened between two planks, from which reaches a hollow square beam placed cross-wise, fastened with cords, to which are added screws; at one end of this stands the engineer, who puts a wooden shaft with a big head into the cavity of the beam; this done two men bend the engine by drawing some wheels : when the top of the head is drawn to the utmost end of the cords, the shaft is driven out of the *ballista*.

BANDALEER, or **BANDELEER**, a large leathern belt, thrown over the right shoulder, and hanging down under the left arm; wore by the ancient musketeers, both for the sustain of their fire-arms, and for the carriage of their musquet-charges; which being put up in little wooden cases, coated with leather, were hung, to the number of twelve, to each *bandaleer*.

The word is originally *French*, *bandouiller*, formed apparently from *bandoalier*, a kind of banditti particularly infesting the *Pyreneans*, who were formerly distinguished by this form of furniture; and were themselves so denominated, *quasi ban de voliers*, a knot of robbers.

The *French* soldiery still retain the bandoleer; their horse, their musqueteers, and common guards, wearing it indifferently; excepting for some difference in its garniture.

BANQUETTE, in fortification, is a little foot-bank, or elevation of earth forming a path which runs along the inside of a parapet; by which the musqueteers get up to discover the counterscarp, or to fire on the enemies in the moat, or in the covert-way. The *banquette* is generally a foot and a half

---

[1] Ammianus Marcellinus (c. 325 – c. 391), was a fourth-century Roman historian.

high, and almost three foot broad : having two or three steps to mount it by. Where the parapet is very high, they make a double *banquette*, one over the other.

BARACK, BARRACK, or **BARAQUE,** a hut or little lodge for soldiers in a camp. Those for the horse were formerly called *baracks*, and those for the foot, *huts*; but *barack* is now used indifferently for both. When the army is in winter quarters they build *baracks*; in the summer they are content with their tents.

Baracks are generally made by fixing four forked poles in the ground; and laying four others across them; afterwards they build up the walls with sods, wattles, or what the place affords; the top is planked, thatched, or covered with turf, as they have convenience.

The word comes from the *Spanish, barracas*, little cabins which fishermen build in the sea shore.

BARRICADE, or **BARRICADO,** a military term for a fence, or retrenchment, hastily made with vessels or baskets of earth, carts, trees, palisades, or the like, to preserve an army from the enemy's shot or assault. The most usual manner of *barricades* is pales or stakes, which are crossed with battoons, and shod with iron at the feet; usually setup in passages, or breaches, to keep back as well the horse as foot. See *Palisade*.

BASTION, in the modern fortification, a huge massive of earth usually faced with sods, sometimes with brick, rarely with stone, standing out from a rampart, whereof it is the principal part. This answers to what in the ancient fortification is called bulwark.

A *bastion* consists of two faces and two flanks. The cases are the lines BC and CS (*Tab. Fort. fig.* 1) including the angle of the *bastion*. The flanks are the lines BA, SD.

The union of the two faces makes the outmost or salient angle, called also the angle of the bastion, BCS. The union of the two faces to the two flanks make the side angles, called *shoulders* or *epaules of the bastion*. And the union of the two other ends of the flanks to the two curtins[1], the angles of the flanks of the *bastion*.

The foundation of a *bastion, i.e.* of a work consisting of flanks and faces, is that great rule in fortification, *viz.* that every part of a work must be seen and defended from some other part : mere angles therefore are not sufficient, but flanks and faces are indispensably requisite. If the bastions EFG and HIK, *fig.* 26. consisted of faces alone, the angles G and H could not be defended from the lines FG or IH. But if the bastion consists of flanks and faces, as ABCSD, it may be defended from the flanks; there being none, *v.gr.* in the face BC, but what may be defended from the opposite flank EL, nor any in

---

[1] Curtin is the archaic spelling for curtain.

the curtin AE, but may be defended from the adjacent flanks BA and EL; nor in any one flank BA, but may be defended from the other BL.

For the proportions of the faces, they are not to be less than twenty-four *Rhineland* perches, nor more than thirty.

The flanks of bastions are better as they are longer, provided they stand at the same angle under the line of defence : hence the flank must stand at right angles to the line of defence. Indeed, in the ancient fortification, the flank is made perpendicular to the curtin so as to have the angle out of the enemy's eye; but this is now provided for by withdrawing the lower part of the flank two or three perches towards the capital line : which part thus withdrawn is better if made concave than rectilinear; and if double, with a ditch between, than single.

The business of disposing the flanks of *bastions* makes the principal part of fortification; it is that on which the defence principally depends, and which has introduced the various forms and manners of fortifying.

If the angle of the *bastion* be less than sixty degrees, it will be too small to give room for guns; and besides, so acute as to be easily beaten down by the enemies guns : to which may be added, that it will either render the line of defence too long, or the flanks too short : it must therefore be more than sixty degrees; but whether or no it should exceed a right angle is still disputed. Hence it follows, that a triangle can never be fortified, in regard either some or all of the angles will be sixty degrees, or less than sixty.

Solid **BASTIONS** are those that are filled up entirely, and have the earth equal to the height of the rampart, without any void space towards the centre.

Void or hollow **BASTIONS** are those surrounded with a rampart and parapet only ranging round their faces, so as to leave a void space towards the centre; where the ground is so low, that if the rampart be taken, no retrenchment can be made in the centre, but what will lie under the fire of the besieged.

Flat **BASTION**, is a *bastion* built on a right line in the middle of a curtin, when it is too long to be defended by the *bastion* at its extremes.

Cut **BASTION**, is that whose point is cut off, and in lieu thereof has a re-entering angle, or an angle inwards with two points outwards; sometimes also called, *bastion* with a tenaille; used either, when, without such a contrivance, the angle would be too acute, or when water or other impediment hinders the carrying on the *bastion* to its full extent.

Composed **BASTION** is when the sides of the interior polygon are very unequal, which makes the gorges also unequal.

Regular **BASTION** is that which has its due proportion of faces, flanks, and gorges; the faces being of an equal length, the flanks the same, and the two angles of the shoulder equal.

Irregular **BASTION** is where this proportion and equality is not observed.

Deformed **BASTION** is where the irregularity of the lines and angles makes the *bastion* out of shape, as when it wants one of its demi-gorges; one side of the interior polygon being too short.

*Demi-***BASTION** is that which hath but one face and one flank; called also an *epaulement*. To fortify the angle of a place that is too acute, they cut off the point, and make two *demi-bastions* which form a tenaille or re-entering angle. Their chief use is before a hornwork or crownwork.

Double **BASTION** is that, which in the plain of the great *bastion*, has another bastion built higher, somewhat after the manner of a cavalier, leaving twelve or eighteen feet between the parapet of the lower and the foot of the higher.

BATTALION, in the military art, a little body of infantry, ranged in form of battle, and ready to engage. A *battalion* usually contains from 5 to 800 men, of which one third were originally pikes in the middle. And the other two thirds musquets posted on the wings : but the number of men it consists of is not determined. *Battalions* are usually drawn up with six men in file, or one before another. Some regiments consist but of one *battalion*.

The word comes from *battle*, an engagement of two armies, &c. and that from *battualia*, the place where two men fight; or from *battalia*, the exercise of people who learned to fight.

BATTERY, in the military art, denotes an eminence cast up, whereon to plant artillery, that it may play to better advantage. The word is *French* formed of *battre*, to beat, strike.

In all *batteries*, the open space left to put the muzzles of the great guns out, are called *embrazures*. The guns are generally about twelve foot distant from one another, that the parapet may be strong, and that the gunners have room to work. There are also *batteries* of mortars, the same with those of cannon, except that they have no merlons[1].

A *battery* of a camp is usually surrounded with a trench and palisades at the bottom, as also with a parapet on the top, having as many holes as there are pieces of artillery, and two redoubts on the wings, or certain places of arms capable of covering the troops who are appointed for their defence.

---

[1] A merlon forms the vertical solid parts of a battlement or crenellated parapet.

Sunk or buried **BATTERY**, is that whole platform is sunk or set down into the ground, with trenches cut in the earth against the muzzles of the guns, to serve for embrazures. This sort, which the *French* call *baterrie en terre*, and *ruinante*, is generally used upon the first making approaches, to beat down the parapet of the place.

*Cross-***BATTERIES**, are two *batteries* at a considerable distance from each other, which play a-thwart one another at the same time, and upon the same point, forming right angles; where, what one bullet shakes, the other beats down.

BATTERY *d'enfilade*, is one which sweeps the whole length of strait line, a street, &c.

BATTERY *en escharpe*, is that which plays obliquely.

BATTERY *de revers*, or murdering *battery*, is one that plays on the back of any place; and being placed on an eminence, sees into it.

BATTERY *joint*, or *par camerade*, or *cameretta*, is when several guns play at the same time upon one place.

BATTERY *en rouage*, is that used to dismount the enemy's cannon.

BATTEURS *d'estrade*, scouts, or horsemen sent out before, and on the wings of an army, two or three miles, to make discoveries; of which they are to give an account to the general.

BATTLE, an action which passes between two armies ranged in order of *battle*, and who engage in a country sufficiently open for them to encounter in front, and at the same time, or at least for the greater part of the line to engage, while the remainder remains in sight, by reason of some difficulty which hinders it from entering so readily into action, with a front equal to that which may be opposed to it by the enemy. Other great actions, though generally of a longer duration, are only called *fights*, by the *French combats*.

    A *battle* lost almost always draws with it the loss of the artillery of the army, and frequently also that of the baggage : consequently, as the army beaten cannot again look the enemy in face till it have repaired those losses, it is forced to leave the enemy a long time master of the country, and at liberty to execute all its schemes. Whereas a great fight lost is rarely attended with a loss of the artillery, and scarce ever of the baggage, because the two armies not meeting in front, they can only have suffered in the part that has been engaged.

    An ingenious modern author remarks, that it is not, usually, the real loss sustained in a *battle* (that is, of some thousands of men) that proves so fatal to a state; but the imaginary loss, and discouragement, which deprives it of the use of those very powers which fortune had left it. *Consid. sur les caus. de la Grand. des Rom.* c. 4. p. 39.

The history of *battles* is only the history of the faults and oversights of generals; luckily enough the mistakes of the two opposite commanders generally balance one another; one of them makes a fault, and the other overlooks, or does not take advantage of it. M. *de Feuquierre's Remarkes sur la Guerre* is little else but a recital of mistakes on both sides; he scarce speaks of one modern general, except *Turenne, Luxembourg,* and the prince of *Condé,* whose conduct was not full of them; *Crequi*[1] and *Catinat*[2] were guilty of great ones which however, they compensated by their judicious conduct on other occasions.

BATTLEMENTS, in the military art, indentures, or notches on the top of a wall, parapet, or other building, in form of embrazures, for the sake of looking through them, &c. much affected in the old fortification.

BERM, in fortification, a small space of ground, four or five foot wide, left without the rampart, between its foot and the side of the moat; to receive the earth that rolls down from the rampart, and prevents its falling into and filling up the moat. This is also called *lisiere, relais, retraite, pas de fouris, foreland,* &c. Sometimes for security the *berm* is palisaded.

BLINDS, or **BLINDES,** in fortification, a sort of defences usually made of oziers, or branches interwoven and laid a-cross, between two rows of stakes, about the height of a man, and four or five foot apart; used particularly at the heads of trenches, when they are extended in front towards the glacis, serving to shelter the workmen, and prevent their being overlooked by the enemy.

BLOCKADE, a sort of a siege of a place, intended to be taken by famine : wherein all the passages, and avenues, are seized and shut up, so as no supplies of provision can be brought in. A *blockade* is no regular siege; inasmuch as there are no trenches or attacks. *Blockades* are formed by the cavalry.

The word *blockade* is sometimes also used in speaking of the beginning of a siege, when forces are sent to seize the principal avenues where the besiegers intend to fix their quarters.

The word comes from the *German blochus,* or *blockhause,* a bulwark, or house of wood; or from the *Gaulish, blocal,* barricade : although others derive from the *Latin buculare,* to stop a passage.

---

[1] Probably Charles I de Blanchefort, Marquis de Créquy, Prince de Poix, Duc de Lesdiguières, (1578–1638), who was a marshal of France.
[2] Nicolas Catinat (1637 – 1712), who was a French military commander and Marshal of France under Louis XIV.

BODY, *corps*, in war, ais an aggregate or assembly of forces, horse and foot, united and marching under some chief. An army, ranged in form of battle, is divided into three *bodies*; the van-guard, the rear-guard, and the main *body*; which last is ordinarily the general's post.

BOMB, a hollow iron ball, filled with gunpowder and furnished with a vent for a fuse, or a wooden tube filled with combustible matter; to be thrown out from a mortar. The word *bomb* comes from the *Latin bombus, crepitus,* or *sibilus ani,* by reason of the noise it makes.

BONNET, in fortification, a kind of little ravelin, without a ditch, having a parapet three foot high; anciently placed before the points of the salient-angles of the glacis, being pallisadoed round : of late also used before the angles of bastions, and the points of ravelins, fausse-brayes. The bonnet has two faces, from ten to fifteen or more rods long : the parapet is made of earth, from thirty to thirty-six foot thick, and from nine to twelve foot high : it is environed with a double row of pallisadoes, ten or twelve paces from each other : hath a parapet three foot high, and is like a little advanced corps de guard.

BONNET *a pestre,* or priest's cap, is an outwork, having at the head three salient angles, and two inwards. It differs from the *double tenaille* only in this, that its sides, instead of being parallel, grow narrower, or closer at the gorge, and open wider at the front; on which account it is also denominated *queue d'aronde,* or swallow's tail.

BOW, *Arcus,* a weapon of offence, made of wood, bone, horn, or other elastic matter, which after being strongly bent, by means of a string fastened to its two ends, in returning to its natural state throws an arrow with great force. It is also called the *long-bow*; by way of distinction from the *cross-bow,* or *arbalet.* The *bow* is most ancient and universal of all weapons. It has been found to obtain among the most barbarous and remote people, and who had the least communication with the rest of mankind. The ancients ascribe its invention to *Apollo.*

The use of the *bow* and arrow was first abolished in *France* under *Louis* XI in 1481; and in their place was introduced the *Swiss* arms, that is, the halbert, pike, and broad-sword.

The *long-bow* was formerly in great vogue in *England*; and many laws were made to regulate and encourage its use. The parliament under *Henry* VIII complain "of the disuse of the *long-bow,* heretofore the safeguard and defence of this kingdom, and the dread and terror of its enemies."

By 33 *H.* 8. c. 9. for every *bow* of yew, the bowyers of *London* were obliged to make two of elm, witch-hazel, ash or other wood; and the country bowyers three. But this law was afterwards repealed so far as related to *London*; and (by 8. *Ed.* c. 10) every bowyer was obliged to have always by him fifty good and able *bows* of elm, witch-hazel, or ash, well and sustainably made and wrought. The best sort of *bows* of outlandish yew not to be sold for above than 6s. 8p. The second sort for 3s. 4p. The course sort, called *livery-bows*, for 2s. By 12. *Ed.* 4. c. 2. that *bows* might not be wanting, nor the price rise too high, every merchant who imported goods from *Venice*, or other place, from which *bow*-staves used to be brought; was for every tun of merchandize to import four *bow*-staves in pain of 6s. 8p. for every *bow*-stave where default is so made. And (by 1. *R.* 3. c. 11) ten *bow*-staves for every butt of malmsey; in pain of 13s. 4p. for every ton.

BREACH, in fortification, is a hole, gap, or aperture, made in any part of the works of a town, either by playing cannon, or springing mines; in order to storm the place, or take it by assault. They say, make good the *breach*; fortify the *breach*; make a lodgment on the *breach* : To clear the *breach* is to remove the ruins, that it may the better be defended. A practicable *breach* is that where the men may mount, and make a lodgment. A *breach* ought to be 15 or 20 fathoms wide. The assailants make their way to it by covering themselves with gabions, earth-bags, &c.

BRIGADE, in the military art, is a party or division of a body of soldiers, whether horse or foot, under the command of a brigadier. There are two sorts of *brigades*, according the *French* way of accounting: 1. A *brigade of an army*, which is a body of horse of ten or twelve squadrons; or of foot, of five or six battalions. And in this way an army is sometimes divided into eight *brigades*, four of horse, and four of foot. 2. A *brigade of a troop* of guards, which is a third part thereof, when the troop consists of fifty soldiers, but only a sixth when it consists of 100; that is, in the former case, the troop is divided into three brigades, in the latter into six.

The word is *French*; some derive it from the *Latin briga*, a *brigue*, or secret intrigue ; *Du Cange*[1] fetches it from *brigand*, an ill-disciplined soldier, who scours the country, and plunders it of every thing, without waiting for the enemy; as the armies of *Arabs*, *Tartars*, &c. The origin of *brigand* is again deduced from *brigandine*, a sort of armour used by the army raised by the *Parisians*, during the captivity of their king *John* in *England*, notorious for their robberies.

BUCKLER, a piece of defensive armour, used by the ancients to screen the bodies from the blows of their enemies. The word comes from the barbarous *Latin bucularium*, of *buccula*, the umbo[2] or middle point of this weapon, which had usually a head or mouth represented prominent thereon.

---

[1] Charles du Fresne, sieur du Cange or Ducange (1610 – 1688), was a French philologist and historian.
[2] The boss or knob at the center of a shield.

The *buckler* of *Achilles* is described by *Homer*, that of *Ænas* in *Virgil*, that of *Hercules* in *Hesiod* : *Ajax's buckler* was lined with seven bulls hides.

The shield succeeded the use of the *buckler*; yet the *Spaniards* still retain the *sword* and *buckler* in their night walks.

Bucklers on medals are either used to signify public vows, rendered to the Gods for the safety of a prince; or that he is esteemed the defender and protector of his people. These were particularly called *votive bucklers*, and were hung at altars, &c.

BULLET, an iron or leaden ball, or shot, wherewith fire-arms are loaded. *Bullets* are of various kinds, *viz. red bullets*, made hot in a forge; intended to set fire to places where combustible matters are found. Some derive the word from the *Latin botellus*, others from the *Greek* βαλλειν, to throw.

According to *Mersenne*[1], a bullet shot, out of a great gun, flies 92 fathom in a second of time, which is equal to 589 ½ *English* feet; and according to *Huygens* would be 25 years in passing from the earth to the sun : but according to some very accurate experiments of Mr. *Derham*[2], it flies, at its first discharge, 510 yards in five half seconds; which is a mile in little above seventeen half seconds : allowing therefore the sun's distance 86051398 *English* miles, a bullet would be 32 years and a half in its passage.

Hollow **BULLETS**, shells made cylindrical, with an aperture and fusee at one end, which giving fire to the inside, when in the ground, it bursts, and has the same effect with a mine.

Chain **BULLETS**, consisting of two balls, joined by a chain three or four foot apart.

Branch **BULLETS**, two balls joined by a bar of iron five or six inches apart.

Two-headed **BULLETS**, called also *angels*, being two halves of a *bullet* joined by a bar or chain : these are chiefly used at sea, for cutting of cords, cables, sails, &c.

---

[1] Marin Mersenne, or Marin Mersennus (1588 – 1648), was a French theologian, philosopher, and mathematician.
[2] William Derham (1657 – 1735), was an English clergyman and natural philosopher.

ℭ

CADET denotes a young gentleman soldier, who to attain some knowledge of the art of war, and in expectation of preferment, chuses to carry arms as a private man in a company of foot. *Cadet* differs from volunteer, as the former takes pay, though only that of a private man, whereas the latter serves without pay. Formerly there were only allowed two *cadets* in each company. In 1682, the king of *France* established companies of *cadets*, wherein the young gentry are trained up to war, and taught the arts and exercises belonging thereto, as riding, fencing, mathematics, &c.

CAMISADE, in the art of war, an attack by surprise in the night, or at the point of day; when the enemy are supposed a-bed. The word is supposed to have took its rise from an attack of this kind; wherein, as a badge, or signal to know one another by, the bore a shift, in *French* called *chemise*, or *camise*, over their arms.

CANNON, in war, a military engine, or fire-arm for throwing iron, lead, or stone bullets, by force of gunpowder, to a place directly opposite to the axis of the cylinder, whereof it consists.

The word seems derived from the *Italian cannone*, an augmentation of *canna*, cane; in regard a *cannon* is long, straight, and hollow like a cane. The first *cannons* were called *bombardae*, from *bombus* by reason of their noise.

The parts and proportions of a *cannon* about eleven foot long are its barrel, or cavity, nine foot; its fulcrum or support, fourteen; and its axis seven; the bore or diameter of the mouth six inches, and two lines the play of the ball : the diameter of the ball therefore six inches; and its weight thirty-three pounds. The metal thick about the mouth two inches, and at the breach six. It weighs about five thousand six hundred pounds : its charge is from eighteen to twenty pounds. It carries, point blank, six hundred paces; and loads ten times in an hour, sometimes fifteen; in a day one hundred and twenty times. Its bed fifteen foot broad, and twenty long for the rebound. It requires twenty horses to draw it.

Larrey[1] makes brass *cannon* the invention of *J. Owen*; and says, the first known in *England*, were in 1535. *Cannons*, however, he owns, were known before; and at the battle of *Cressi*, in 1346, there were five pieces of *cannon* in the *English* army; which were the first that had been seen in *France* :

---

[1] Possibly Isaac de Larrey, Sieur de Grandchamp et de Courménil (1639 - 1719), who was a French historian.

Mezeray[1] adds, that king *Edward* struck terror into the *French* army; it being the first time they had seen such thundering machines.

Cannons are made cylindrical, that the motion of the ball may not be retarded in its passage; and that the powder, when on fire, might not slip between the ball and the surface of the *cannon* which would hinder its effect. *Wolfius[2]* would always have the *cannon* decrease towards the mouth or orifice : in regard, the force of the powder always decreases in proportion to the space in which it is expanded.

The new *cannons*, after the *Spanish* manner, have a cavity or chamber at the bottom of the barrel, which helps their effect. A *cannon* is found to recoil two or three paces after explosion; which some account for from the air's rushing violently into the cavity as soon as it is discharged of the ball : but the real cause is the powder's acting equally on the breech of the *cannon* and the ball.

For a battering piece, whose ball is thirty-six pounds, there must be two cannonneers, three charges, and thirty pioneers.

Cannons are distinguished from the diameters of the balls they carry; but this distinction is different in different nations. The proportion of their length to their diameter depends rather on experience, rather than any reasoning *a priori*; and has been accordingly various, at various times and places; the rule is, that the gun be of such a length, as that the whole charge of powder be on fire ere the ball quit the piece. If it be made too long, the quantity of air to be driven out before the ball will give too much resistance to the impulse; and that impulse ceasing, the friction of the ball against the surface of the piece will take off some of its motion.

Formerly, *cannons* were made much longer than at present; till some made by chance 2½ foot shorter than ordinary, taught them that the ball moves with a greater impulse through a less space than a longer. This *Gustavus* king of *Sweden* proved in 1624; when an iron ball, forty-eight pounds weight, was found to go further from a new short *cannon* than another ball of ninety-six pounds out of an older longer piece : whereas, in other respects, it is certain the larger the bore and ball, the greater the range.

The greatest range of a *cannon* is ordinarily fixed at an elevation of 45°. Dr. *Halley[3]* shews it to be 44 1/2. M. *St. Julien[4]* adjusts the ranges of several pieces of *cannon*, from the weight of the ball they bear; the charge of gunpowder being always supposed in a subduple ratio of the ball. The same

---

[1] François Eudes de Mézeray (1610 – 1683), who was a French historian.
[2] Probably Christian Wolff, also known as Wolfius (1679 – 1754), who was a German philosopher.
[3] Edmond Halley, (1656 – 1742), was an English astronomer, geophysicist, mathematician, meteorologist, and member of the Royal Society.
[4] Possibly Franz Xaver Johann Nepomuk Graf Saint-Julien und Walsee, or François-Xavier de Guyard, comte de Saint-Julien (1756 - 1836), who was an Austrian infantry commander during the French Revolutionary Wars.

author adds, that a ball thrown to the distance of six hundred paces, sinks nine, ten, eleven, twelve, nay, thirteen foot within the ground.

For the metal of *cannons*, it is either iron, or, which is more useful, a mixture of cooper, tin and brass : the tin is added to the copper to make the metal more dense and compact; so that the better and heavier the copper is, the less tin is required. Some to an hundred pounds of copper, add ten of tin, and eight of brass, and ten of lead. *Braudius* describes a manner of making *cannon* of leather, on occasion : and it is certain the *Swedes* made use of such in the long war of the last century; but these burst too easily to have much effect. It is found by experience, that of two *cannons* of equal bore, but different lengths, the longer requires a greater charge of powder than the shorter, in order to reach the same range. The ordinary charge of a *cannon* is for the weight of its gun-powder to be half that of its ball. After each thirty discharges, the *cannon* is to be cooled with two pints of vinegar, mixed with four of water, poured into the barrel; the touch-hole being first stopped.

CAPONIERE, in fortification, a covered lodgment, sunk four or five foot into the ground, encompassed with a little parapet about two foot high, serving to support several planks covered with earth. The *caponiere* is large enough to contain fifteen to twenty soldiers, and is usually placed on the glacis at the extremity of the counterscarp, and in dry moats; having little embrasures for the soldiers to fire through.

CAPTAIN, a military officer, whereof there are various kinds, and degrees; distinguished by their commands : as,

CAPTAIN *of a Company*, or *Troop*, is an inferior office, who commands a company of foot, or troop horse, under the colonel. In the like sense we say a *captain* of dragoons, of granadiers, of marines, of invalids, &c. In the horse and foot guards, *captains* are styled *colonel*, being usually persons of rank, and general officers of the army. In the colonel's company of a regiment, *i.e.* the first company, or that whereof he himself is *captain*, the commanding office is called *captain lieutenant*.

Lieutenant **CAPTAIN**, is the *captain's* second, or the officer who commands the company under the *captain*, and in his absence. In some companies, &c. he is called *captain lieutenant*.

CAPTAIN *Lieutenant*, is he who commands a company, or troop, in the name and place of some other person, who has the commission, with the title, honour, and pay thereof; but is dispensed withal, on account of his quality, from performing the function of his post.

Thus, the colonel, being likewise the *captain* of the first company of his regiment; that company is commanded by his deputy, under the title of *captain lieutenant*.

So in *England, France,* &. the king, queen, prince, dauphin, &c. have usually the titles, dignities, &c. of *captains* of the guards, the real duty of which offices are performed by *captain lieutenants.*

Reformed **CAPTAIN**, is one, who upon a reduction of the forces, has his commission and company suppressed; yet is continued *captain*, either as a second to another, or without any post of command at all.

CAPTAIN *Bashaw*, signifies the *Turkish* high-admiral.

CAPTAIN *General*, of an army, is the general, or commander in chief.

CAPTAIN *of Militia*, he who commands a company of trained bands, or troop of light horse.

CARABINE, a small sort of fire-arm, shorter than the fusil, and carrying a ball of twenty four in the pound; born by the light horse, hanging at a belt over the left shoulder. The *carabine* is a kind of medium between the pistol and the musquet; and bears a near affinity to the harquebuss, only that its bore is smaller. It was formerly made with match lock, but of late only with a flint lock. The barrel is two foot and a half long, and is sometimes furrowed spirally within, which is said to add to the range of the piece.

CARABINEERS, a sort of light horse, carrying longer *carabines* than the rest; and used sometimes on foot. The *French*, of late days, have formed entire corps of these *carabineers*, which cannot have but good effect; this being a sort of soldiery chosen out of the whole cavalry, and better paid than the rest. There are said to be none in the *English* army but in major-general *Windham's* regiment.

CARCASSE, or **CARCUSS**, in war, a kind of bomb, usually oblong, or oval, rarely circular; consisting of a shell or case, sometimes of iron, with holes; more commonly of a coarse string canvas, pitched over, and girt with iron hoops; filled with combustible matters, as hand grenados, ends of musquets, loaden pistols, and preparations of gunpowder, &c. Its use is to be thrown out of a mortar, to set houses on fire, and do other execution. It has the name *carcasse* because the circles which pass from one ring, or plate, to the other seem to represent the ribs of a human carcass.

CARTOUCHE, a wooden case, about three inches thick, girt round with marlin, and loaden with two, three or four hundred musket balls, besides six or eight balls of iron of a pound weight; to be fired out of a hobit, or small sort of mortar, chiefly for the defence of pass or the like. The *Cartouche* is also called by the *French Gargouge, Gargouche,* or *Gargousse.*

In cannon of casemates or other posts, which defend the passage of the ditch, *Cartouches* have a terrible effect : since bursting asunder they spread the shot they are loaden with far and wide. There are divers others forms and compositions of *Cartouches*, some made for guns, &c.

CARTOUCHE is also used for what is more frequently called a *Cartridge*.

CARTRIDGE, in the military art, the charge or load of a fire-arm, wrapped in a thick paper, or pastboard, parchment; to be more readily charged, or conveyed into the piece. *Cartridges* are the same with what the *French* call *Cartouches*, from which word *Skinner* scruples not to derive *Cartridge*.

Those of cannon and mortar are usually of pastboard, or tin, sometimes of wood, half a foot long; taking up the place of the bullet of the piece, to whose caliber the diameter is proportioned. Those of muskets, pistols, and small arms, only contain the charge of powder, with a ball wrapped up in thick paper.

CASERNS, or **CAZERNS**, in fortification, little rooms, or huts, erected between the ramparts, and the houses of fortified towns, or even on the ramparts themselves; to serve as lodging for the soldiers of the garrison, to ease the garrison. There are usually two beds in each *casern*, for six soldiers to lie, who mounts the guard alternately; the third part being always on duty.

CASE-SHOT, are musquet bullets, stones, old pieces of iron, or the like put up into cases, and so shot out of great guns. *Case-shot* is chiefly used at sea, to clear the enemies decks when they are full of men.

CASTRAMETATION, the art or act of incamping, *i.e.* of placing and disposing an army in camp. The word is more used in speaking of the incampments of the ancients than those of the moderns. It comes from the *Latin castrum*, camp, and *metari*, to measure or layout.

CAVALIER, or **CAVALEER**, a horseman or person mounted on horse-back : especially if he be armed withal, and have a military appearance. Anciently, the word was restrained to a knight or *miles*. The *French* still use *Chevalier* in the same sense.

CAVALIER, in fortification, is a mound, or elevation of earth, either round or oblong; having a platform on the top, bordered with a parapet, to cover the cannon placed on it, and cut with embrasures to fire through; serving to overlook and command all around the place.

Cavaliers are raised in sieges on the bastions and curtins of ramparts, in order to fire on the eminences around, and oblige the enemy to get further off, as well as to scour the trenches. But the gorge of the bastion is the place where *Cavaliers* are most properly erected; those raised on the curtin being rather called *Platforms*.

CAVALRY, a body of soldiers who fight or march on horseback. The word comes from the *French cavalerie*, and that from the corrupt *Latin caballus*; whence *Caballerius* and *Cavallerius* in the later *Latin*, and καβλλερος in the *Greek*.

The *cavalry* is usually divided into horse and dragoons. The horse are either regimental or independent troops; to which latter sort belong the horse-guards, and in *France*, the gendarmes and musketeers who serve on horseback. The dragoons and regimental horse form what they call the *Light Cavalry* : the trooper the *Heavy Cavalry*. When an army is ranged in battle, the *Cavalry* are posted on the wings. Bodies of *Cavalry*, ranged in form of battle, are called *Squadrons*.

CAVIN, in the military art, a natural hollow fit to cover a body of troops, and hereby facilitate their approach to a place. A *Cavin* near a place besieged is of great advantage to the besiegers; as by help thereof they can open trenches, make places of arms, keep guards of horse and the like without being exposed to the enemies shot.

CAZEMATE, in fortification, a kind of vault or arch of stone-work, in that part of the flank of a bastion next the curtin; somewhat retired or drawn back towards the capital of the bastion; serving as a battery to defend the face of the opposite bastion, and the moat, or ditch.

The name comes from a vault, formerly made to separate the platforms of the upper and lower batteries; each of which was called in *Italian Casa Armata*, and in the *Spanish Casamata*. Though others derive the word from *Casa a Matti*, house of fools; *Covarruvius* from *casa* and *mata*, low house.

The *Cazemate* sometimes consists of three platforms, one above another; the highest being on the rampart : but they commonly consent themselves to withdraw the last within the bastion.

The *Cazemate* is also called the *low place*, and *low flank*, as being at the bottom of the wall next the ditch; sometimes *retired flank*, as being that part of the flank nearest the curtin, and the centre of the bastion : it was formerly covered with an epaulement, or a massive body either round or square; which prevented those without from seeing within the batteries; whence it was also called *covered flank*.

It is now rarely used, the enemies batteries are apt to bury the artillery of the *casemate* in the ruins of the vault; besides, that the terrible smoak made by the discharge of the cannon makes intolerable to the men. Hence instead of the ancient covered *cazemates*, later engineers have contrived open ones, only guarded by a parapet, &c.

CENTER *of a Bastion*, is a point in the middle of the gorge of the bastion, whence the capital line commences, and which is ordinarily at the angle of the inner polygon of the figure.

CENTRY *Box*, a wooden cell or lodge, made to shelter the sentinel, or sentry, from the injuries of the weather. In a fortification, such lodges are usually placed on the flanked angles of the bastions, on those of the shoulder, and sometimes in the middle of the curtain.

CHAMADE, in war, a certain beat of drum, or sound of a trumpet, which is given to the enemy as a signal, to inform them of some proposition to be made to the commander; either to capitulate, or have leave to bury their dead, make a truce or the like. *Menage*[1] derives the word from the *Italian Chiamata*, of *clamare*, to cry.

CHAMBER *in War*, is used for the place where the powder of the mine is lodged.

CHAMBER *of the Mortar*, or *Cannon* of the new make, is a cell or cavity at the bottom of the barrel, or chace, where the powder is lodged. The different form of the chamber, is found by experiment, to have an influence on the range of a piece. A cubical chamber carries the ball to a less distance than a circular one; and that less than a cylindrical one.

CHARGE, in gunnery, the load of a piece, or the quantity of powder and ball, or shot, wherewith it is prepared for execution. The weight of gunpowder necessary for a charge is commonly in a subduple proportion to that of the ball.

The rules for *charging* large pieces in war, are, that the piece be cleaned or scoured within side; that the proper quantity of gunpowder be next driven in and rammed down; care, however, being taken that the powder be not bruised in ramming, which weakens its effect; that a little quantity of paper, hay, or the like, be rammed over it, and that then the ball or shot be intruded.

If the ball be red-hot, a tampion, or trencher of green wood, to be driven in before it.

CIRCUMVALLATION, in fortification, a line or trench, with a parapet, thrown up by the besiegers, encompassing all their camp, to defend it against any army that may attempt to relieve the place.

The word is formed from the *Latin circum*, about, and *vallum*, wall or mound.

The line is to be cannon-shot distance from the place, ordinarily about twelve foot broad, and seven deep. It is bordered with a breast-work, and

---

[1] Gilles Ménage (1613 – 1692), was a French scholar.

flanked with redoubts, or little forts, erected from space to space. It serves both to prevent any succour being sent into the place, to keep deserters, and prevent incursions of the enemies garrison.

Care must be taken that the line of *circumvallation* never pass by the foot of an eminence; less the enemy seizing on the eminence, lodge his cannons and command the line.

CITADEL, or **CITTADEL**, a fort, or place fortified with four, five, or six bastions; built sometimes in the most eminent part of a city, and sometimes only near the city. In the first case, the citadel serves to defend the city against enemies. In the latter, it serves to command it, and to keep the inhabitants in their obedience : for which reason the city is left unfortified on the part toward the *Citadel*, but the *Citadel* is fortified towards the city.

The most usual form for *Citadels* is the pentagon; a square being too weak, and a hexagon too big. There is always a large esplanade between the city and the *Citadel*.

The word is a diminutive of the *Latin citta*, city, *q.d.* little city.

COFFER, in fortification, denotes a hollow lodgment, athwart a dry moat, from six to seven foot deep, and from sixteen to eighteen foot broad; the upper part made of pieces of timber raised two foot above the level of the moat; which little elevation has hurdles laden with earth for its covering; and serves as a parapet with embrasures.

The *Coffer* is nearly the same with the caponiere, abating that this last is sometimes made beyond the counterscarp on the glacis, and the *Coffer* always in the moat, taking up its whole breadth, which the caponiere does not. It differs from the transverse and gallery, in that these latter are made by the besiegers, and the *Coffer* by the besieged.

The besieged generally made use of *Coffers* to repulse the besiegers when they endeavour to pass the ditch. To save themselves from the fire of those *Coffers*, the besiegers throw up the earth on that side of the *Coffer*.

COLONEL, an officer in the army, who has the command in chief of a regiment, either of horse, foot or dragoons. *Skinner* derives the word from colony, being of the opinion, the chiefs of colonies called *colonials* might give the name to chiefs of forces. In the *French* and *Spanish* armies, *Colonel* is confined to the infantry and dragoons : the commanding officer of a regiment of horse, they usually call *mestre de camp*.

COLONEL-LIEUTENANT, is he who commands a regiment of guards, whereof the king, prince, or other person of the first eminence is *colonel*. These *colonels lieutenants* have always a colonel's commission, and are usually general officers.

LIEUTENANT-COLONEL, is the second officer in the regiment; who is at the head of the captains, and commands in the absence of the *colonel. Lieutenant-colonel* of the horse or dragoons is the first captain of the regiment.

COMBAT, in a general sense, denotes an engagement; or a difference decided by way of arms. Authors distinguish in an army between a *combat* and a battle; the latter expressing the general action of the whole army, the former a particular skirmish, or engagement of a single part; so that the *combat* is properly a part of the battle.

COMMANDING *Ground*, in fortification, an eminence or rising ground which overlooks any post or strong place. Of this they reckon three sorts: 1°. A *front commanding ground*; which is an height opposite to the face of the post, which plays upon its front. 2°. A *reverse commanding ground*, which is an eminence which can play upon the back of any place or post. 3°. An *enfilade commanding ground*, or *curtin commanding ground*, which is an high place, that can with its shot scour all the length of a straight line.

CORBEIL, in fortification, little baskets about a foot and a half high, eight inches wide at the bottom, and twelve at the top : which being filled with earth, which are frequently set upon against another on the parapet, or elsewhere; leaving certain port-holes, whence to fire upon the enemy under covert, without being seen by them.

CORDON, in fortification, a row of stone jutting out between the rampart and the basis of the parapet, like the tore[1] of a column. The *cordon* ranges round the whole fortress; and serves to join the rampart, which is aslope, and the parapet, which is perpendicular, more agreeably together. In fortifications raised of earth, this space is filled up with pointed stakes instead of a *cordon*.

CORIDOR, or **CORRIDOR**, in fortification, a road or way along the edge of the ditch, withoutside; encompassing the whole fortification. It is also called the *covert way*; because covered with a glacis, or esplanade, serving it as a parapet. The *corridor* is about twenty yards broad. The word comes from the *Italian coridore*, or the *Spanish corridor*

CORNET, in the modern war, denotes an officer in the cavalry, who carries the ensign or colours of a troop. The *cornet* is the third officer in the company, and commands in the absence of the captain and lieutenant. He takes his title from his ensign which is square, and is supposed to be called by that name, from *cornu*; because placed on the wings which form a kind of points or horns of the army. Others derive the name from *coronet*; alledging

---

[1] The lowest molding at the base of a column.

that it was the ancient custom for these officers to wear *coronets* or garlands on their heads.

CORNICHE *ring* of a piece of ordnance, is that which lies next the trunnion ring, or the next ring from the muzzle backwards,

CORPORAL, in inferior officer in a company of foot, who has charge over one of the divisions, places and relieves sentinels, and keeps good order in the *corps de garde*; receiving, withal, the word, of the inferior rounds that pass by his *corps de garde*. There are usually three *corporals* in each company. The word comes from the *Italian corporale*, which signifies the same thing; and that from *caput*, head, chief; the *corporal* being the first of the company.

CORPS *de garde*, a post in an army, sometimes under covert, sometimes in the open air, to receive a body of soldiery, who are relieved from time to time, and are to watch in their turns for the security of a quarter, a camp, station, &c.

CORPS *de Bataille*, is the main body of an army drawn up for battle.

COVERT *Way*, in fortification, is a space of ground level with the adjoining country, on the edge of the ditch, ranging quite round the half-moons, and other works withoutside the ditch. It is otherwise called corridor, and hath a parapet together with its banquette and glacis, which form the height of the parapet. This is also sometimes called the counterscarp, because it is on the edge of the scarp.
    One of the greatest difficulties in a siege is to make a lodgment on the *covert way*; because, usually, the besieged palisade it along the middle, and undermine it on all sides.

COUNTER-APPROACHES, in fortification, lines or trenches made by the besieged when they come out to attack the lines of the besiegers in form.

Line of **COUNTER-APPROACH**, a trench which the besieged make from their covered way to the right and left of the attacks, in order to scour or enfilade the enemies works. It should commence in the angle of the place of arms of the half moon that is not attacked, and of the bastion that is attacked; about 50 or 60 fathoms from the attacks; and continued as far as will be found necessary in order to see the enemy in his trenches and parallels. This line must be perfectly enfiladed from the covered way and the half moon, that if the enemy get possession of it, it may be of no service to him. In this line the governor must frequently in the night-time send small parties of horse or foot to drive the workmen from their posts; and if possible carry off the engineers, who have the direction of the works.

COUNTER-BATTERY, a battery raised to play on another in order to dismount the guns.

COUNTER-BREAST-WORK, in fortification, see *fausse-braye*.

COUNTER-MARCH, in war, a change of face, or wings of the battalion, whereby the men who were in the front come to be in the rear. This is an expedient they have recourse to when the enemy attacks their rear; or where they change their march to a direction opposite to that wherein they had begun. The *counter-march* is either made by files or ranks; by files, when the men in the front of the battalion go into the rear; by ranks, when the ranks, or wings, of the battalion change ground with one another. The term is also used at sea for the like change or motion of a squadron of ships.

COUNTER-MINE, in war, a subterranean vault, running the whole length of a wall, three foot broad and six deep, with several holes and apertures therein; contrived to prevent the effect of mines, in case the enemy should make any to blow up the wall. This kind of *counter-mine* is now little in use. The modern *counter-mine* is a well or pit, and a gallery, sunk on purpose till it meet the enemy's mine, and prevent its effect : it being first pretty well known whereabouts it is.

COUNTER-SCARP, in fortification, the exterior slope, or acclivity of the ditch, looking towards the campaign. See *Tab. Fortification, fig.* 21.

COUNTER-SCARP, is also used for the covert-way, and the glacis. *Counter-scarps* are sometimes made of stone and without any slope. *To be lodged on the counter-scarp,* is be lodged on the covert-way or glacis.

COUNTER-SWALLOW-TAIL, in an outwork, is the form of a single tenaille, wider at the gorge,

COUNTER-TRENCH, in fortification, a trench made against the besiegers, and which, of consequence, has its parapet turned towards them. There is usually a great many communications between this and the place, to prevent the enemy from making any use of it, in case they render themselves masters thereof.

COUNTER-VALLATION, a *counter*-line, or ditch, made around a place besieged, to prevent the sallies and excursions of the garrison, when it is strong. Along its edge, on the side of the place, runs a parapet; and it is flanked from space to space.

CROISADE, CRUZADE, or **CRUZADO**, a *holy war*, or an expedition against infidels and heretics; particularly against the *Turks*, for the recovery of *Palestine*. People anciently flocked on these *croisades* out of devotion; the pope's bull, and the preaching of the priests of those days, making it appear a point of conscience. Hence several orders of knighthood took their rise.

Those who meant to go on this errand, distinguished themselves with crosses of different colours, wore on their clothes; and were thence called *croises*; the *English* wore them white; the *French* red; the *Flemish* green; the *Germans* black; and the *Italians* yellow.

They reckon eight *croisades* for the conquest of the holy land : the first undertaken in 1095, at the council of *Claremont*; the second in 1144, under *Louis* VII; the third in 1188, by *Henry* II of *England*, and *Philip Augustus* of *France*; the fourth in 1195, by pope *Celestin* IV and emperor *Henry* VI; the fifth published in 1198, by order of pope *Innocent* III, wherein the *French, Germans*, and *Venetians* engaged; the sixth, under the same pope, began tumultuarily, in 1213, and ended in the rout of the Christians; the seventh resolved at the council of *Lyons*, in 1245, undertaken by S. *Louis*; the eighth, which was the second of S. *Louis*, and the last of all, in 1268.

It is said, it was the *Cistercian* monks who first projected the *croisades*; *Philip Augustus* solicited the execution of thereof with the holy see; and *Innocent* III raised the first standard of the cross. It was the council of *Claremont* who ordered that they who embarked herein should bear the cross in their banner; and those that entered themselves into the service, should also wear it on their clothes.

Towards the middle of the twelfth century, there was also a croisade of the *Saxons* against the pagans of the north; wherein the archbishop of *Magdeburg*, the bishops of *Halberstadt, Munster, Mersburgh, Branden-burgh*, &c. with several lay-lords embarked. And towards the beginning of the same century, under the pontificate of *Innocent*, there was also a *croisade* undertaken against the *Albigenses*; where were become powerful in *Languedoc*, &c.

CROWN-WORK, in fortification, an outwork running into the field; designed to keep off the enemy, gain some hill or advantageous post, and cover the other works of the place. See *Tab. Fortif. fig.* 21. The *crown-work* consists of two demi-bastions at the extremes, and an entire bastion on the middle, with curtins.

CROWNED *horn-work*, is a *horn-work* with a *crown-work* before it. See *Horn-Work*.

CULVERIN, a long slender piece of ordnance or artillery, serving to carry a ball to a great distance. Of these there are three kinds, *viz.* the *culverin extraordinary*, the *ordinary*, and the *least sized*.

The *culverin extraordinary* has 5½ inches bore; its length 32 calibers, or 13 foot; weighs 4800 pounds; its load above twelve pound; carries a shot 5 inches 1/4 diameter, weighting 20 pound weight.

The *ordinary culverin* is twelve foot long; carries a ball of 17 pound 5 ounces; caliber 5½ inches; its weight 4500 pound.

The culverin of the least sized, has its diameter 5 inches; is 12 foot long; weighing about 4000 pounds; carries a shot 3½ inches diameter, weighing 14 pounds 9 ounces.

Menage derives the word from the *Latin colubrina*; others from *colubra* snake; either on account of the length and slenderness of the piece, or the ravages it makes.

CUNETTE, or **CUVETTE**, in fortification, a deep trench, about three or four fathom wide, sunk along the middle of a dry moat, to lade out the water; or to make the passage more difficult to the enemy.

CURTIN, CURTAIN, or **COURTINE**, in fortification, that part of a wall, or rampart, which is between two bastions, or which joins the flanks thereof.

Du Cange derives the word from the *Latin cortina, quasi minor cortis*, a little country court; he says, it was in imitation hereof, that they gave this name to the walls and parapets of cities, which inclose them like courts : he adds, that the *curtains* of beds take their name from the same origin; that *cortis* was the name of the general's or principal's tent; and that those who guarded it we called *cortinarii* and *curtisani*.

The *curtin* is usually bordered with a parapet five foot high; behind which the soldiers stand to fire upon the covert way and into the moat.

Besiegers seldom carry on their attacks against the *curtin*; because it is the best flanked of any part.

𝕯

DEFILE, in fortification, a narrow pass, or way, through which a company of horse, or foot, can pass only in file, by making a small front, so that the enemy may make an opportunity to stop their march, and to charge them with so much the more advantage, in regard that the front and rear cannot reciprocally come to the relief of one another. The word is formed from the *French defile*, to unthread, or unstring.

DEMI-BASTION, is a kind of fortification, that has only one face and one flank.

DEMI-CANNON, a piece of ordnance, usually about 6 inches bore, 5400 pound weight, 10 or 11 foot long, and carrying a shot of 30 or 32 pound weight. It carries point blank 150 paces; its charge of powder 14 pound weight.
    There also two sizes of *Demi-Cannon* above this, which are something larger : as, the *ordinary Demi-Cannon*, which is 6 inches ½ bore, 12 foot long, weighs 6500 pound; its charge of powder 17 pounds 8 ounces, carries a shot 6 ounce and a half in diameter, and whose weight is 32 pound : this piece shoots blank 162 paces.
    Demi-Cannon of the largest size is 6 inches 6/8 bore, 12 foot long, 600 pound weight; its charge is 18 pound weight of powder, and it carries 180 paces.

DEMI-CULVERING, is a piece of ordnance commonly 4 ½ inches bore, 10 foot long, 2700 pound weight; its charge is 7 pound 4 ounces of powder, and it carried a shot of 10 pound 11 ounces; and shoots point blank 174 paces. *Demi-Culvering of the largest sort*, is 5 inches 6/8 bore, 10 foot long; its charge of powder is 8 pound and 8 ounces; the ball is 4 ½ inches diameter, weights 12 pound 11 ounces; and the point blank shoot 178 paces.

DEMI-GORGE, in fortification, is half the gorge, or entrance into the bastion; not taken directly from angle to angle, where the bastion joins to the curtin; but from the angle of the flank to the centre of the bastion or angle the two curtins would make, were they thus protracted to meet in the bastion.

DEMI-LUNE, Half-Moon, in fortification, an outwork as EFGHK (*Tab. Fortif. fig.* 3) consisting of two faces, and two little flanks; frequently built before the angle of a bastion, and sometimes also before the curtin, though now much disused. The gorge terminates in a crescent or half-moon, whence the denomination *Demi-Lune*.

DESCENT *into a Ditch*, is a deep ditch or sap cut through the esplanade, and under the covert way; covered overhead with planks and hurdles; and loaded with earth against artificial fires. In wet ditches the *Descent* is made even with the surface of the water : in dry ditches it is carried to the bottom of the moat; where traverses are made to lodge and secure the miners, &c.

DESERTER, in war, a soldier on the muster roll who quits the service without leave; or lists himself under another officer in a different regiment. The punishment of *Desertion* is death. All soldiers found half a league from a garrison, or army, going towards an enemy's country, or quarter, without a pass, are deemed and treated as *Deserters*. The ancient church excommunicated *Deserters* as having violated their oath.

DETACHED *Pieces*, in fortification, demi-lunes, ravelins, horn and crown-works, and even bastions when separated, or at a distance from the body of the place.

DETACHMENT, a military term, signifying a number of soldiers, taken out of several regiments or companies equally, to be employed in some particular enterprize; as to form a kind of flying camp, to relieve a party already engaged in battle, to join a separate army, to assist at the siege of a place, or to enter into some garrison, &c.

DISARMING, the act of depriving a person of the use or possession of arms. On the conclusion of a peace, it is usual for both sides to *disarm*. We have divers laws for *disarming* papists and all recusants. Under king *George* I a law was made for *disarming* the highlanders; none of whom, except peers, or gentlemen of 100 *l. per ann. Scots* are to wear any arms, in the field, on the road, or at market.

The game law[1] has, in effect, disarmed all the common people of *England*, under 100 a year in landed estate, except the servants of lords of manors. Yet by the ancient policy of *England* the whole nation was obliged to bear arms.

DITCH, in fortification, called also *Foss* and *Moat*, a trench dug around the rampart or wall of a fortified place, between the scarp and counterscarp. Some *Ditches* are dry; others full of water : each whereof have their advantages. The earth dug out of the ditch serves to form the rampart.

---

[1] The Game Act passed in 1671 stated that all persons unqualified to hunt, at least 95% of the population, were not qualified to keep or bear arms.

The *Ditch* should be of such breadth that the tallest tree may not reach over it, *i.e.* from 15 to 20 fathoms; though the rule others give for the dimensions of the *Ditch*, is, that if afford earth enough to build the rampart of due magnitude. The space between the rampart and *Ditch*, being about 6 foot, is called the *Berm*, or *List*.

DONJON, in fortification, generally denotes a large strong tower, or redoubt of a fortress, where the garrison may retreat in case of necessity, and capitulate with greater advantage. See *Dungeon*.

DUNGEON, DONJON, in fortification, the highest part of a castle built after the ancient mode; serving as a watch-tower, or place of observation. In some castles, as that of *Vincennes*, &c. the *Donjon* serves as a prison for persons they would have the most securely kept; whence the use of our word *Dungeon*, for a dark close prison under ground.

The word comes from the *French Donjon*, which signifies the same; and which *Fauchet* derives from *Domicilium*, in that the *Dungeon* being the strongest part of the castle, was usually the lord's apartment. *Menage* derives it from *Dominione*, or *Dominionus*, which in some ancient writings we find used in the same sense. Others derive it from *Domus Julii Caesaris*, or *Domus Jugi*; and others from *Domus Juliani*, the emperor *Julian* having built several such castles in the *Gauls*, whereof there is one still standing in *Lorraine*, called *Dom. Julian*.

𝕰

ENFANS PERDU, a *French* phrase, used in war, to signify the soldiers who march at the head of a body of forces appointed to sustain them; in order to begin an attack, make an assault, or force a post. The word literally imports *lost children* on account of the imminent danger they are exposed to. In *English* they are called the *forlorn*, or *forlorn hope*. At present it is with the grenadiers that usually begin such attacks.

ENFILADE, in war, is applied to trenches and other lines which are ranged in a right line, and so may be scoured, or swept by the cannon lengthwise, or in the direction of the line, and rendered almost defenceless.

Care must be taken that the line be not *enfiled*, or *enfiladed* : on the contrary, the covert line must be *enfiladed*, that the enemy may be driven out of it. The last boyau, or gut of the trenches, is subject to be *enfiladed*, that is, to be scoured according to its length.

A *battery d'enfilade* is that where the cannon sweep a right line. A *post*, or *command d'enfilade*, is a height from which one may sweep a whole right line at once.

ENSIGN, in the military art, a banner, or colours, under which the soldiers are ranged, according to the different companies, or parties they belong to.

The *Turkish* ensigns are horsetails; those of the *Europeans*, are pieces of taffety, with divers figures, colours, arms, and devises thereon. *Xenophon* tells us, that the ensign bore by the *Persians* was a golden eagle on a white flag; the *Corinthians* bore the winged horse, or *Pegasus*, in theirs; the *Athenians* an owl; the *Messenians* the *Greek* letter M; the *Lacedaemonians* the Λ.

The *Romans* had a great diversity of *ensigns*; the wolf, minotaur, horse, boar, and at length the eagle, where they stopped; this was first assumed in the second year of the consulate of *Marius*.

ENSIGN is also used for an officer in the infantry who bears the *ensign* or colours; by the *Latins* called *signifier*, and *vexillifer*. He has charge of the *ensign* in battle; and if he be killed the captain is to take it in his stead. The *ensign* is under command of the lieutenant, and in his absence supplies his post.

ENVELOPE, in fortification, a mount of earth, sometimes raised in the ditch of a place, and sometimes beyond it; being either in form of a simple parapet, or of a small rampart bordered with a rampart. These *envelopes* are made where weak places are only to be covered with single lines; without advancing towards the field; which cannot be done but by works which require a great deal of room; such as horn-works, half-moon, &c. *Envelopes* are sometimes called *sillons, contregards, conserves, lunettes,* &c.

EPAULE, or **ESPAULE**, in fortification, the shoulder of the bastion; or the angle made by the face and the flank; otherwise called the *angle of the epaule*. The word is pure *French* and literally implies *shoulder*.

EPAULEMENT, in fortification, a side-work hastily thrown up to cover the cannon or the men. It is made either of earth thrown up, of bags filled with sand or earth, or of gabions, fascines, &c. with earth : of which latter sort the *epaulements* of the places of arms,, for the cavalry, behind the trenches, usually are.

EPAULEMENT is also used for a demi-bastion, consisting of a face and flank, placed at the point of a horn or crown-work. Also, for a little flank, added to the sides of a horn-work, to defend them when too long. Also, for the redoubts made on a right line to fortify it. And, lastly, for an orillon, or mass of earth almost square, faced and lined with a wall, and designed to cover the cannon of a casemate.

ESCALADE, or **SCALADE**, a furious attack of a wall or a rampart; carried on with ladders to mount by; without proceeding in form, breaking ground, or carrying on works to secure the men.

ESCOUADE, is usually the third part of a company of foot; so divided for mounting guards, and for the more convenient relieving one another. It is equivalent to a brigade of a troop horse.

ESPLANADE, in fortification, called also *glacis*; a part which serves the counterscarp, or covert way, for a parapet; being a declivity, or slope of earth, commencing from the top of the counterscarp, and losing itself insensibly in the level of the campaign.

ESTRADE, a *French* term, literally signifying a public road or high-way. Hence the military phrase, *battre l'estrade*, or *beat the estrade*, that is, to send scouts, or horse-men, to get intelligence, to learn the dispositions of the enemy, and inform the general of every thing like to fall in the way. An army never marches without sending *batteurs d'estrade* on every side.

The word is formed of the *Italian strada*, street, or road, which is derived from the *Latin strata*, a paved street. Some derive it from *estradios*, who were cavaliers anciently employed in *beating the estrade*.

ETAPPE, in war, an allowance of provisions, and forage made to the soldiers, upon march through a kingdom or province, to or from winter quarters. Hence, he that contracts with the country, or territory, for furnishing the troops, is called *etappier*.

𝔉

FASCINES, in fortification, small branches of trees, or bavins, bound up in bundles; which being mixed with earth, serve to fill up ditches, screen the men, make the parapets of trenches, &c. See *Tab. Fortif. fig.* 24.

Some of them are dipped in melted pitch or tar; and being set on fire, serve to burn the enemy's lodgments or other works. A pitched *Fascine* is a foot and a half about : a *Fascine* for defence, two or three foot.

In the corrupt *Latin* they use *Fascenina*, *Fascennia*, and *Fascinata*, to signify the pales, *Fascines*, &c, used to enclose the ancient castles, &c.

FAUCON, or **FALCON**, a small piece of cannon, whose diameter is 2 ¾ inches; weight, 750 pound; length, 7 foot; load, 2 ¼ pound; shot, 2 ½ inches diameter, and 2 ½ pound weight.

FAUCONET, or **FALCONET**, a very small piece of ordnance, whose diameter at the bore is 2 ¼ inches; weight, 400 pound; length, 6 foot; load, 1 ¼ pound; shot, something more than 2 inches in diameter; and 1 1/8 pound weight.

FAUSSE-BRAYE, in fortification, an elevation of earth, two or three fathoms broad, round the foot of the rampart on the outside, defended by a parapet which parts it from the berme, and the edge of the ditch : its use is for the defence of the ditch. The *Fausse-braye* is the same which is otherwise called the *Chemins des rondes*, & *Basse enceinte*, &c.

It is of little use where ramparts are faced with wall, because of the rubbish the cannon beats down into it. For this reason, engineers will have none before the faces of the bastions, where the breech is commonly made; because the ruins falling, the *Fausse-braye* makes the ascent to the breech the easier : besides that which flies from the faces kills the soldiers placed to defend it.

FIELD-*pieces*, are small cannon, usually carried along with an army in the *field* : such as three pounders, minions, sakers, six pounders, demi-culverins, and twelve pounders; which being light and small are easily carried.

FIELD-*staff*, is a staff carried by the gunners : it is about the length of a halbert, having a spear at the end, which in each side has ears screwed on, like the cock of a match-lock. In these the gunners screw lighted matches when they are on command; which is called arming the *field-staffs*.

FIELD-*works*, in fortification, are those thrown up by an army, in the besieging of a fortress; or else by the besieged in defence of the place. Such are the fortifications of camps, of highways, &c.

FIGURE, in fortification, is the plan of the fortified place or the interior polygon. When he sides and angles are equal it is called a *regular*, when unequal, an *irregular figure*.

FLANK, in war, is used by way of analogy, for the side of a battalion, army, &c. in contra-distinction to the Front and Rear. *To attack the enemy in Flank*, is to discover and fire upon them on one side. The enemy took us in *Flank* : the *Flank* of the infantry must be covered by the wings of the cavalry.

FLANK, in fortification, is a line drawn from the extremity of the face towards the inside of the work. Such is the line B A *Tab. Fortif. fig.* 1. Or, *Flank* is that part of the bastion, which reaches from the curtin to the face, and defends the opposite face, *Flank*, and the curtin.

Oblique, or *second* **FLANK**, is that part of the curtin, intercepted, between the greater line of defence, and the lesser : and from which they can see to scour the face of the opposite bastion.

Low, covered, or *retired* **FLANK**, is the platform of the casemate, which lies hid in the bastion : otherwise called *orillon*.

FLANK *Fitchant* is that from which a cannon playing, fireth its bullets directly in the face of the opposite bastion.

FLANK *Razant* is the point from whence the line of defence begins, from the conjunction of which with the curtin, the shot only raseth the face of the next bastion; which happens when the face cannot be discovered from the *Flank* alone.

Simple **FLANK** are lines going from the angle of the shoulder to the curtin; whose chief office is for defence of the moat, and place.

FLANKED *Angle*, in fortification, is the angle formed by the two faces of the bastion, and which of course forms the point of the bastion.

FLANKED *Tenaille*. See *Tenaille*.

FLANKING, in the general, is the act of discovering and firing upon the side of a place, body, battalion, &c. The *flank* a place is to dispose a bastion, or other work in such manner, as that there shall be no part of the place, but what may be defended, *i.e.* may be played on both in front and rear.

To *flank* a wall with towers. This bastion is *flanked* by the opposite *flank*, and a half-moon. This horn-work is *flanked* by the curtin.

Any fortification that has no defence but just right forwards is faulty : and to render it complete, one part ought to be made to *flank* the other. Hence the curtain is the strongest part of any place, because it is *flanked* at each end.

Battalions are also said to be *flanked* by the wings of the cavalry. A house is sometimes said to be *flanked* by two pavilions, or two galleries; meaning it has a gallery, &c. on each side.

FOOT-BANK, or **FOOT-STEP**, *Banquette*, in fortification, is a small step of earth, on which the soldiers stand to fire over the parapet.

FORT, a little castle, or fortress; or a place of small extent, fortified by art, or nature, or both. A *Fort* is work encompassed around with a moat, rampart, and parapet; to secure some high ground, or passage of a river; to make good an advantageous post; to fortify the lines and quarters of a siege, &c.

Royal **FORT**, is a *Fort* whose line of defence is at least twenty-six fathoms long.

Star **FORT**, is a sconce, or redoubt, constituted by re-entering and salient anglers; having commonly from five to eight points; and the sides flanking each other.

FORTIFICATION, called also *military architecture*, is the art of fortifying, or strengthening a place; by making works around the same, to render it capable of being defended by a small force, against the attacks of a more numerous enemy. Some authors go back to the beginning of the world for the author and origin of military architecture. According to them God himself was the first engineer; and paradise, or the *Garden of Eden* the first fortress. But however ancient soever the surrounding of cities, will walls, towers, &c. may be, the name *Fortification* and the art now understood thereby, are of no very old standing.

They had their rise since the invention of cannons; the terrible effects whereon rendered it necessary to change the structure of the ancient walls, and add so many things thereto, that those changes were thought to constitute a new art, which was called *Fortification* by reason of the strength it afforded to those in cities, to defend them against an enemy.

The first authors who have wrote of *Fortification*, considered as a particular formed art, are *Ramelli*[1] and *Cataneo*[2], *Italians*. After them *Errard*[3], engineer to *Henry* the great of *France*; *Stevinus*[4], engineer to the prince of *Orange*, *Marolois*[5], the chevalier *de Ville*[6], *Lorini*[7], *Cohorn*[8], the count *de Pagan*[9], and the marshal *de Vaubin*[10] : which last two authors contributed greatly to the perfection of the art.

From the idea and office of *Fortification*, some general fundamental rules or axioms may be drawn : as,

1° That the manner of *fortifying* should be accommodated to that of attacking : So that no one manner can be assured will always hold, unless it be assured the manner of besieging be incapable of being altered; and to judge of the perfection of a *Fortification*, the manner of besieging at the time it was built must be considered.

2° All the parts of a *Fortification* should be able to resist the most forcible machines used for besieging.

3° A *Fortification* should be so contrived as that it may be defended with as few men as possible; which consideration, when well attended to, save a world of expence.

4° That the defendants may be in the better condition, they must not be exposed to the enemies guns and mortars; but the aggressors be exposed to theirs.

Hence, 5° All the parts of a *Fortification* should be so disposed as that they may defend each other; in order to this, every part there is to be flanked, *i.e.* capable of being seen and defended from some other; so that there be no place where an enemy can lodge himself, either unseen, or under shelter.

6° All the campaign around must lie open to the defendants; so that no hills or eminences must be allowed, behind which the enemy might shelter himself from the guns of the *Fortification*; or from which he might annoy

---

[1] Agostino Ramelli (1531–ca. 1610), who was an Italian engineer.
[2] Pietro Cataneo or Cattaneo (ca. 1510 - ca. 1574), who was an Italian military arhictect.
[3] Jean Errard (ca. 1554 - 1610), who was a French mathematician and military engineer.
[4] Simon Stevin (1548 – 1620), was a Flemish mathematician and military engineer.
[5] Samuel Marolois, Marollois, Maroloys or Marlois (1572 - 1627), who was a Dutch mathematician and military engineer.
[6] Antoine de Ville (1596-1656), who was a French military engineer.
[7] Buonaiuto Lorini (1540 - 1611), who was an Italian military engineer.
[8] Menno, Baron van Coehoorn (1641 – 1704), was a Dutch soldier and military engineer.
[9] Blaise Pagan (1604 - 1665), who was a French army engineer and founded France's first fortification school.
[10] Sébastien Le Prestre de Vauban, Seigneur de Vauban and Marquis de Vauban (1633 – 1707), was a Marshal of France and military engineer.

them with his own. The fortress then is to command all the place round about; consequently the outworks must all be lower than the body of the place.

7° No line of defence to be above point blank musket shot, which is about one hundred and 20 fathom.

8° The acuter the angle at the centre, the stronger is the place; as consisting of more sides, and consequently more defensible.

Such are the general laws and views of *Fortification* : the particular ones, respecting each several work or member thereof, will be delivered under their proper articles.

FORTIFICATION is also used for the place *fortified*; or the several works raised to defend and flank it, and keep off the enemy. All *Fortifications* consist of lines and angles which have various names according to their various offices.

The principle angles are those of the *centre*, the *flanking* angle, *flanked* angle, angle of the *epaule*, &c.

The principal lines are those of *circumvallation*, of *contravallation*, of the capital, &c.

Fortifications are divided into *regular*, and *irregular*; and again into *durable* and *temporary*.

Regular **FORTIFICATION**, is that wherein the bastions are all equal; or that built in a regular polygon; the sides and angles whereof are generally about a musket shot from each other. In a regular *Fortification*, the parts being all equal, have the advantage of being equally defensible; so that there are no weak places.

Irregular **FORTIFCATION**, is that wherein the bastions are unequal and unlike; or the sides and angles not all equal and equidistant. In an irregular *Fortification*, the defence and strength being unequal; there is a necessity for reducing the irregular figure, as near as may be, to a regular one.

And, as the irregularity of a figure depends on the quantity of angles and sides; the irregularity of a *Fortification* arises either from the angles being too small, or the sides being too long or too short.

Consequently, an irregular figure being proposed to be fortified; all the angles, with the quantity of the sides; must be found, to be able to judge how it is to be fortified.

Durable **FORTIFICATION**, is that built with design to remain a standing shelter for ages. Such are the usual *Fortifications* of cities, frontier places, &c.

Temporary **FORTIFICATION**, is that erected on some emergent occasion and for a little time. Such are field-works, cast up for the seizing and maintaining a post, or passage; those about camps, &c. as circumvallations, contravallations, redoubts, trenches, batteries, &c.

The methods of fortifying that have been invented are various; and new methods continue still to be proposed. The principal, and those which chiefly obtain through *Europe*, are those of *Coehorn*, *Pagan*, *Vaubin*, and *Scheiter*, from which all the rest are easily conceived.

FORTIN, or **FORTLET**, a diminutive of the word *Fort*, importing a little *Fort*, or sconce, called also *Field Fort*, built in haste, for defence of a pass or post; but particularly to defend a camp in the time of a siege; where the principal quarters are usually joined, or made to communicate with each other by lines defended by *Fortins* and redoubts.

Fortins being very small, their flanked angles are generally one hundred and twenty fathom distant from each other; but their figure and extant are various according to the place and occasion; some having whole bastions, and others only half bastions.

FOSS, or **FOSSE**, in fortification, a moat or ditch. The word is *French*, formed of the *Latin* participle *fossum*, of the verb *fodio*, I dig.

FOUGADE, or **FOUGASSE**, in the art of war; a little mine, in a manner of a well, scarce exceeding ten foot in width, and twelve in depth; dug under some work, or post that is like to be lost; and charge with barrels or sacks of gunpowder, covered with earth. It is set on fire, like other mines, with a saucisse. The word is *French* : M. *Huet*[1] derives it from *focata*, of *focus*, fire. fire.

FRAISE, in fortification, a kind of defence, consisting of point stakes, driven parallel to the horizon, into the retrenchments of a camp, a half moon, or the like, to fend off and prevent any approach or scalade.

FUZEE, **FUZE**, of **FUSE**, in war, an appendage of a bomb, or granado-shell; by which the powder or composition in the shell is set on fire to do the designed executions. The word is *French* a literally denotes a spindle.

The *fusee* is wood pipe or tap filled with wild-fire or the like composition; and is designed to burn so long, and no longer, as is the time of the motion of the bomb from the mouth of the mortar to the place where it is to fall : which times is about twenty-seven seconds : so that the *Fusee* must be contrived, either from the nature of the composition, or the length of the pipe which contains it, to burn just that time. The usual composition of *Fusees* is two ounces of nitre, to one of sulphur, and three of gunpowder dust.

---

[1] Possibly Pierre Daniel Huet (1630 – 1721), who was a French churchman and scholar.

𝕲

GABIONS, in fortification, &c. large baskets, made of osier twigs, woven of a cylindrical form, six foot high, and four wide; which being filled with earth, serve as a defence, or shelter from the enemies fire. See *Tab. Fortif. fig.* 19. They are commonly used in batteries to screen the engineers, &c. in order to which one is placed on each side of the gun, only leaving room for the muzzle to appear through.

There are also a smaller sort of *Gabions*, used on parapets, in trenches, &c. being placed so close as that a musquet can just peep through.

To render the *Gabions* useless they endeavour to set them on fire by throwing pitched faggots among them.

GALLERY, in fortification, a covered walk, or passage made a-cross the ditch of a town besieged, with timbers fastened on the ground, and planked over. The sides of the *Gallery* are to be musquet proof, and consist of a double row of planks, lined with plates of iron; and the top is sometimes covered with earth, or turf, to hinder the effects of the stones, artificial fires, &c. of the enemy.

Galleries are chiefly used to secure and facilitate the miners approach to the face of the bastion, over the moat, which is already supposed filled up with faggots and bavins, and the artillery of the opposite flank dismounted. Sometimes it is called a *Traverse*.

GALLERY *of a mine*, denotes the *branch*; or that narrow passage under ground, leading to a mine carrying on under any work designed to be blown up. The besiegers and besieged do each of them carry *Galleries*, or branches under ground, in search of each other's mines, which sometimes meet and destroy each other.

GALLOGLASSES, a kind of militia, or soldiery, in Ireland. *Camden*[1], in his annals of *Ireland*, p. 792. relates that the militia consist of cavalry, or horsemen, called *Galloglasses*, or *Galloglassii*, who use a very sharp sort of hatchet; and infantry called *Kerns*.

GARRISON, a body of forces, disposed in a fortress, to defend it against the enemy; or to keep the inhabitants in subjection; or even to be subsisted

---

[1] William Camden (1551 – 1623) was an English antiquarian, historian, topographer, and officer of arms.

during the winter season. *Du Cange* derives the word from the corrupt *Latin garnisio*, which the later writers use to signify all manner of munitions, arms, victuals, &c.

Garrison and *winter-quarters* are sometimes used indifferently for the same thing; and sometimes they denote different things. In the latter case, *garrison* is a place wherein forces are maintained, to secure it; where they keep regular guard : as a frontier town, citadel, castle, tower, &c. The garrison should always be stronger than the towns-men. *Winter-quarters* signify a place where a number of forces are laid up in the winter season, without keeping the regular guard. The soldiers like better to be in *winter-quarters* than in *garrison*.

GAZONS, in fortification, turfs, or pieces of fresh earth covered in fresh grass, cut in form of a wedge, about a foot long, and half a foot wide : to line or face works made of earth, in order to keep up the same, and prevent their mouldering.

GENERAL *officers*, in an army, are those who do not only command over a single company or regiment; but whole office and authority extends over a body of several horse and foot. Such are lieutenant-generals, major-generals, generals of the horse, of the foot; paymaster-general, commissary-general, chirurgeon-general, muster-master-general, &c.

The term is also now used in a more extensive sense; and comprehends such as may command, by virtue of their rank, several bodies of force, though all of the same kind. In which sense brigadiers are *general* officers; notwithstanding that they are attached to one kind of forces, either infantry or cavalry.

GENERALISSIMO, also called *Captain-General*, and simply the *General*; is an officer who commands all the military powers of a nation; who gives orders to all the other generals; and receives no orders himself but from the king. Mons. *Balzac* observes, that the cardinal *de Richelieu* first coined this word, of his own absolute authority, upon his going to command the *French* army in *Italy*.

GLACIS, in fortification, is particularly used for that of the counterscarp; being a sloping bank that reaches from the parapet of the counterscarp, or covert way, to the level side of the field. See *Tab. Herald. fig.* 21. The *glacis*, otherwise called the *esplanade*, is about six foot high, and loses itself by an insensible diminution in the space of ten fathoms.

The **GORGE** *of a Bastion*, is what remains of the sides of the polygon of a place, after retrenching the curtins : in which case it makes an angle in the centre of the bastion. Such A H D *Tab. Fortif. fig.* 1. In flat bastions the *gorge* is a right line on the curtin reaching between the two flanks.

GORGE *of a half-moon*, or *ravelin*, is the space between the ends of their two faces next the place. *Gorge* of the other out-works is the interval betwixt their sides next the ditch. All the *gorges* are to be destitute of parapets; otherwise, besiegers having taken possession of a work, might make use thereof to defend themselves from the shot of the place : so that they are only fortified with palisadoes, to prevent a surprise.

Half the **GORGE**, *demi* **GORGE**, that part of the polygon between the flank, and the centre of the bastion. See *Demi-Gorge*.

GRANADIER, GRENADIER, or **GRANADEER**, a soldier armed with a sword, fire-lock slung, and a pouch full of hand-granadoes to be thrown among the enemy. There are companies of *foot-granadiers*, and *horse granadiers*, or *granadiers* of horse, by the *French* called *granadiers volans*, or *flying granadiers*, who are mounted on horseback but fight on foot.

Every company of foot, of late years, has generally a company of *granadiers* belonging to it; or else four or five *granadiers* belong to each company of the battalion; which, on occasion, are drawn out and form a company of themselves. These always take the right of the battalion; and the first in attacks.

To each group of horse-guards, *Chamberlayn*[1] tells us, there is added, by establishment, a troop of *granadiers* of sixty-four men, beside officers, command by the captain of the troop of guard.

One division of *granadiers* mounts with a division of the troop; go out on small parties from the guard; perform sentinels duty, &c.

GRENADO, or **GRENADA**, in the military art, a hollow all or shell of iron, brass, or even glass, or potters earth, filled with gunpowder, and fitted to a fuze to give it fire. The name *granado* takes its rise hence, that it is filled with grains of powder, as a pomegranate is with kernels. Of these there are two kinds the one large, the other small : the first to be thrown at the enemy by a mortar, properly called *bombs*. The latter to be cast with the hand, and thence denominated *hand-grenadoes*.

Casimir[2], indeed, makes another distinction; where the ball or shell is round, whatever the size be, he calls it a *grenado*, and where oval or cylindrical, a *bomb* : but custom allows only the former division.

The best way, *Casimir* observes, to secure a man's self from the effects of the *grenado* is to lie flat down on the ground before it burst.

---

[1] Probably Edward Chamberlayne (1616 – 1703), who was an English writer.
[2] Probably Kazimierz Siemienowicz (ca. 1600 - ca. 1651), who was a Polish-Lithuanian general of artillery, gunsmith, military engineer, and artillery specialist.

Historians relate, that at the siege of *Ostend* there were above fifty thousand *grenadoes* thrown in one month into the city; and that the citizens threw above twenty thousand into the works of the besiegers.

The common, or *hand-grenado*, is a little hollow ball of iron, tin, wood, pastboard, &c. filled with strong powder, lighted with a fuzee, and thus thrown by hand into places where men stand thick; and particularly into trenches and lodgments.

Their composition is the same with that of *bombs* : which see. For size they are usually about the bigness of an iron bullet, and weight about three pounds: as to dimensions, they are commonly of a thickness one eighth, one ninth, or one tenth of their diameter; their aperture or orifice about 8/19 wide, as prescribed by *Casimir*.

Thuanus[1] observes, the first time *grenadoes* were used was at the siege of *Wachtendonk*, a town near *Gueldres*; and that the inventor was an inhabitant of *Velno*, who in making an experiment in the effect thereof, occasioned two thirds of that city to be burnt, the fire being kindled by the fall of a *grenado*.

Bombs were known long before the invention of *grenadoes*. The ancients had a sort of *ollae*, or fire-pots, somewhat of the same nature with our *grenadoes*, but less perfect.

Casimir mentions a kind of blind *grenadoes*, without any aperture or fuzee, as not needing to be lighted; but being thrown with a mortar, take fire of themselves whenever they fall on any hard solid object.

GUARD, in the military sense, is properly the duty or service done by the soldiers to secure the army or place from the attempts and surprizes of the enemy. Of this there are divers kinds as,

Advanced **GUARD**, a party of horse or foot which marches before a corps to give notice of approaching danger. When an army is on the march, the grand *guards*, which should mount that day, serve as an *advanced guard* to the army. That small body also of fifteen to twenty horse, commanded by a lieutenant, beyond, but within sight of the main, or before the grand *guard* of the camp, are called the *advanced guard*.

Grand **GUARD**, consists of three or four squadrons of horse, commanded by a field officer, and posted before the camp on the right and left wing, towards the enemy; for the security of the camp. In a camp, every battalion posts a small guard, commanded by a subaltern officer, about one hundred yards before its front. This is called a *quarter guard*. That small *guard* of foot, which a regiment mounts in their front, under a corporal, is called the *standard-guard*.

---

[1] Jacques Auguste de Thou (1553 – 1617), was a French historian, book collector and president of the Parlement of Paris.

Main **GUARD**, is that from which all the other *guards* are detached. Those who are to mount the main *guard*, meet at the respective quarters, and from thence go to the parade; where, after the whole *guard* is drawn up, the small *guards* are detached for the posts and magazines; and then the subaltern officer draws lots for their *guards*; and are commanded by the captain of the main *guard*.

Piquet **GUARD**, is a number of horse and foot, who keep themselves always in a readiness in case of alarm; the horses being saddled, and the riders booted all the while : the foot draw up at the head of the battalion at the beating of the tattoo, but afterwards return to their tents, where they remain in a readiness to march on any sudden alarm. This *guard* is to make resistance, in case of an attack, till the army can get ready.

GUERITE, in fortification, a centry box; being a small tower of wood or stone, placed usually on the point of a bastion, or on the angles of the shoulder; to hold a centinel, who is to take care of the ditch, and watch out against a surprize.

GUN, a fire-arm, or weapon of offence, which forcibly discharges a ball, shot, or other offensive matter, through a cylindrical barrel, by means of gunpowder. *Gun* is a general name, under which is included divers, or even most species of fire-arms. They may be divided into *great* and *small*.

Great **GUNS**, called by the general name cannon, make what we also call ordnance, or artillery; under which come the several sorts of cannon, as cannon-royal, demi-cannon, &c. culverins, demi-culverins, sakers, minions, falcons, &c.

Small **GUNS**, include muskets, musketoons, carabines, blunderbusses, fowling-pieces, &c. Pistols and mortars are almost the only kinds of regular weapons charge with gunpowder that are excepted from the denomination of *Guns*.

GUNNERS, officers of the tower, and other garrisons, whose business is to manage and look after the ordnance mounted on the lines, and batteries, which are all fixed and ready with cartouches and ball, for service on the shortest warning. One or more of them are on duty day and night; they carry a field staff, and a large powder horn on a string over the left shoulder : in which equipage they march by the guns.

GUNNERY, the art of shooting with guns and mortars, *i.e.* of charging, directing, and exploding those fire-arms to the best advantage. See *Tab. Fortif. fig.* 16. *Gunnery* is sometimes considered part of the military art, and sometimes of pyrotechny.

To the art of *gunnery* belongs the knowledge of the force and effect of gunpowder, the dimensions of pieces and the proportions of the powder and ball they carry; with the methods of managing, charging, pointing, spunging, &c.

Some parts of *gunnery* are brought under mathematical consideration, which, among mathematicians are called absolutely by the name *gunnery*, *viz.* the method of elevating or raising the piece to any given angle, and of computing its range; or of raising and directing it so it may hit a mark or object proposed. The instruments chiefly used in this part of *gunnery*, are the calipers, or gunners compasses, quadrant, and level.

The line or path in which the bullet flies, whatever direction or elevation the piece is in, is found to be the same as that with all other projectiles, *viz.* a parabola.

Maltus, an *English* engineer, is mentioned as the person who first taught any regular use of mortars in the year 1634; but all his knowledge was experimental and tentative; he knew nothing of the curve the shot describes n its passage, nor of the difference of range at different elevations. And most of the gunners and engineers employed about batteries, &c. to this day go by no better rules; if the range does not hit right, they raise or lower the piece till they bring to a truth : and yet there are certain rules, founded on geometry, for all these things : most of which we owe to *Galileo*, engineer to the grand duke of *Tuscany*, and his disciple *Torricellius*.

H

HALBARD, or **HALBERT**, an offensive weapon, consisting of a shaft or staff, five foot long; with a steel head, somewhat in manner of a crescent. The *halbard* was anciently a common weapon in the army; where there were companies of *halbardeers* : it is still carried by the serjeants of foot, and dragoons.

It was called the *Danish* ax, because first bore by the *Danes*, and on the left shoulder. From the *Danes* it was derived to the *Scots*; and from the *Scots* to the *English Sax*ons; and from them to the *French*.

The word is formed of the *German hal*, hall, and *bard*, an hatchet. *Vossius* derives if from the *German* hellebaert, of *hel*, clarus, splendens, and *baert*, ax.

HALF-MOON, *Demi Lune*, in fortification, an outwork consisting of two faces, forming together a salient angle, whose gorger is turned like a *half moon*. *Half moons* are sometimes raised before the curtin, when the ditch is wider than it ought to be; in which case it is much the same with a ravelin; only that the gorge of a *half-moon* is made bending in like a bow, or crescent, and is chiefly used to cover the point of the bastion; where ravelins are always placed before the curtin. But they are both defective as being ill flanked.

HARQUEBUSS, in our ancient statutes, called also *Arquebuse, Haquebut*, or *Hagbut*; is a hand-gun; or a firearm of a proper length, &c. to be bore in the arm. The *haquebuss* is properly a fire-arm, of the ordinary length of a musket, or fowling-piece; cocked usually with a wheel. *Hanzelet*[1] prescribes its legitimate length to be forty calibers; and the weight of its ball, one ounce and seven-eighths; its charge of powder as much.

There is also a larger kind, called *harquebuss a croc*, much of the nature of our blunderbusses, used in war, for the defence of places; being usually rested on something when discharge.

The first time these instruments were seen was in the imperial army at *Bourbon*, who drove *Bonivet*[2] out of the state of *Milan*. They were so big and heavy there were two men to carry them. They are now little used, except in some old castles, and by the French in some of their garrisons.

---

[1] Jean Appier-Hanzelet, (1596-1647), who was a French engraver and illustrator, and published books on artillery and pyrotechnics.
[2] Guillaume Gouffier, seigneur de Bonnivet (ca. 1488 – 1525), was a French soldier.

The word is formed of the *French arquebuse* : and that from the *Italian arcobuso*, or *arco abuso*, of *arco*, a bow, and *busio*, a hole; on account of the touch-hole, at which the powder is put to prime it; and that it succeeded to the bows of the ancients.

HENDECAGON, in fortification, is taken for place defended by eleven bastions.

HEPTAGON, in fortification, a place strengthened with seven bastions for its defence.

HERRISON, in fortification, a beam armed with iron spikes, the points whereof are turned outward; supported in the middle by a stake, wherein is a pivot on which it turns; and serving as a barrier to block up a passage. *Herrisons* are frequently placed before gates; especially the posterns of a town or fortress, to secure those passages, which of necessity be frequently opened and shut.

HERSE, in fortification, a lattice, or port-cullice, in form of an harrow[1]; beset with iron spikes. It is usually hung by a rope fastened to a moulinet[2]; to be cut, in case of surprize, or when the first gate is broken with a petard; that the *herse* may fall, and stop up the passage of the gate, or other entrance of a fortress.

The *herse* is otherwise called a *sarrasin*, or *cataract*; and when it consists of straight stakes, without any cross-pieces, it is called *orgues*.

The word *herse* is *French*, and literally signifies a harrow; being formed of the *Latin herpex*, or *irpax*, which denote the same.

HERSE, is also a harrow, which the besieged, for want of *chevaux de frise*[3], lay in the way, or in breeches, with pints up, to incommode the march as well of the horse, as the infantry.

HERSILLON, in the military art, a sort of plank, or beam, ten or twelve foot long, whose two sides are drove full of spikes, or nails, to incommode the march of the infantry or cavalry. The word is a diminutive of *herse*; the *hersillon* doing the office of a little *herse*.

HEXAGON, in fortification, is a fortress with six bastions. See *Bastions*.

---

[1] A harrow is a gate made of timber, whose dimensions are commonly 6 by 4 inches; and 6 inches distant from each other, well fastened to three or four cross bars, and secured with iron.
[2] A drum upon which the rope is wound in a capstan, crane, etc.
[3] The cheval de frise was a defensive anti-cavalry measure consisting of a portable frame (sometimes just a simple log) covered with many projecting long iron or wooden spikes.

HOBITS, a sort of small mortars, from six to eight inches diameter, mounted on carriages, made after the gun fashion; used for annoying the enemy at a distance with small bombs

HOLLOW *Tower*, in fortification, is a rounding made of the remainder of two brisures[1], to join the curtin to the orillon : where the small shot are played, that they may not be so much exposed to the enemy.

HORN-WORK, in fortification, a sort of out-work, advancing toward the field, to cover and defend a curtin, bastion, or other place supposed to be weaker than the rest; as also to possess a heighth, &c. See *Tab. Fortif. fig.* 21. *lit. f.* It consists of two demi-bastions, joined by a curtin. Its sides or flanks are usually parallel; though sometimes they approach or contract toward the place, forming what they call a *queue d'aronde*, or swallows tail. See *Queue d'aronde.*

HORSE, is also used in the military language, to express the cavalry; or body of soldiers who serve on horse-back. The army consisted of 30000 foot and 10000 *horse*. The *horse* includes *horse*-guards, *horse*-grenadiers, and troopers. Dragoons are also frequently comprehended under the under the name, although they fight on foot.

Horse guards, by the *Spaniards* called *guardas a cavallo*; by the *French gardes de corps*; and by the *English* usually *life-guards*; are guards of the king's person and body, consisting of 800 men, well armed and equipped. They are divided into four troops; to which are now added, by establishment, two troops of granadiers, consisting of 80 men, all under the command of a captain.

Each troop of *horse* guards is divided into four divisions or squadrons; two of which, consisting of 100 men, commanded by a principal commissioned officer, two brigadiers, and two sub-brigadiers, with two trumpets, mount the guard, one day in six, and are relived in their turns. Their duty is, by parties of the guard, to attend the king's person when he goes out near home. When he goes out of town, he is attended by detachments out of all the three troops.

One division of granadiers mounts with a division of the troops to which they belong; and go out on small parties from the guard, perform centinel duty on foot, attend the king also on foot, &c.

Light **HORSE** includes all the *horse* except the life-guard. The term *light horse* is also sometimes applied to an independent troop; or a troop not embodied in a regiment. The denomination arose hence, that anciently they were lightly armed, in comparison of the royal guards, which were armed at all points.

---

[1] A brisure is any part of a rampart or parapet which deviates from the general direction.

HORSE-SHOE, in fortification, is a work sometimes of a round, sometimes of an oval figure, inclosed with a parapet, raised in the ditch of a marshy place, or in low grounds; sometimes also to cover a gate; or to serve as lodgment for soldiers, to prevent surprizes, or relieve an over tedious defence.

HURDLES, in fortification, twigs of willows or osiers, interwoven close together, sustained by string stakes, and usually laden with earth. *Hurdles*, called also *clayes*, serve to render batteries firm, to consolidate the passages over muddy ditches, to cover traverses, and lodgments for the defence of the workmen against the artificial fires or stones that may be cast upon them.

HUSSARS, HUSSARDS, or **HUSSARTS**, on order or species of soldiery in *Poland* and *Hungary*, commonly opposed to the *Ottoman* cavalry. The *hussars* are horsemen, clothed in tigers or other skins, and garnished and set out with plumes of feathers. Their arms are the sabre and bayonet. They are very resolute; firm partisans : and better in a hasty expedition than a set battle. The emperor and king of *France* have of these *hussars* in their service.

J

INSCONSED, in the military art, denotes that a part of an army have fortified themselves with a sconce, or small fort, in order to defend some pass, &c.

INSULT, a military term used for the attack of any post with open force; without the apparatus of trenches, saps, or any regular approaches.

J

JANIZARIES, an order of infantry in the *Turkish* army; reputed the grand seignior's foot guard.

Vossius[1] derives the word from *genizers*, which, in the *Turkish* language, signifies *novi homines*, or *milites*; *d'Herbelot*[2] tells us, *jenitcheri* signifies a *new band*, or troop; and that the name was first given by *Amurath* I, called the Conqueror, who chusing out one fifth part of the Christian prisoners, whom he had taken from the *Greeks*, and instructing them in the discipline of war, sent them to *Hagi Bektasche* (a person whose pretended piety rendered him revered among the *Turks*) to the end he might confer his blessing on them, and at the same time give them some mark to distinguish them from the rest of the troops. *Bektasche*, after blessing them in his manner, cut off one of the sleeves of the fur gown he had on, and put it on the head of the leader of this new militia; from which time, *viz.* the year of Christ 1361, they have still retained the name *jenitcheri*, and the fur cap.

As, in the *Turkish* army, the *English* troops are distinguished from those of *Asia*; the *janizeries* are also distinguished into *janizeries* of *Constantinople*, and of *Damascus*. Their pay is from two aspers to twelve per diem; for when they have a child, or do any signal piece of service, their pay is augmented.

Their dress consists of a dolyman, or long gown, with short sleeves, which is given them annually by the grand seignior on the first day of *Ramazan*. They wear no turban, but in lieu of that a kind of cap, which they call *zarcola*, and long hood of the same stuff hanging on their shoulders. On solemn days they are adorned with feathers, which are stuck in a little case on the fore part of the bonnet.

Their arms, in *Europe*, in times of war, are a sabre, a carabine or musquet, and a cartouche-box hanging on the left side. At *Constantinople*, in times of peace, they wear only a long staff in their hand. In *Asia*, where powder and fire-arms are more uncommon, they wear a bow and arrows, with a poignard, which they call *haniare*.

The *janizeries* where heretofore a body formidable even to their masters, the grand seigniors : *Osman*, they first stripped of his empire, and afterwards of his life; and sultan *Ibrahim* they deposed, and at last strangled in the castle of the Seven towers : but they are now much less considerable. Their number is, or ought to be, fixed at twenty thousand.

---

[1] Gerrit Janszoon Vos (1577 – 1649), also known by Gerardus Vossius, was a Dutch classical scholar and theologian.
[2] Barthélemy d'Herbelot de Molainville (1625 – 1695), was a French Orientalist.

The *janizeries* are children of tribute, levied by the *Turks* among the Christians, and bred up to military life. They are taken at the age of twelve years, to the end, forgetting their country and religion, they may know no other parent but the sultan. However, generally speaking, they are not now-a-days raised by way of tribute; for the *carach*, or tax, which the *Turks* impose on the Christians, for allowing them the liberty of their religion, is now paid in money; excepting in some places, where money being scarce, the people are unable to pay in specie, as in *Mingrelia* and other provinces near the Black sea.

The officer who commands the whole body of *janizeries* is called *janizar agasi*; in *English*, *aga* of the *janizeries*; who is one of the chief officers of the empire.

Though the *janizeries* are not prohibited marriage, yet they rarely, marry nor then, but with the consent of their officers; as imagining a married man to make a worse soldier than a bachelor.

It was *Osman*, or *Ottoman*, or, as others will have it, *Amurath*, who first instituted the order of *janizeries*. They were are first called *jaja*, that is, footmen, to distinguish them from the other *Turks*, the troops whereof consisted mostly of cavalry.

Vigenere[1] tells us, that the discipline observed among the *janizeries* is extremely conformable, in a great many things, to that used in the *Roman* legions.

JUST, or **JOUST**, a sportive kind of combat on horseback, man against man, armed with lances. Anciently, *justs* and tournaments made up a part of the entertainment at all solemn feasts and rejoicings. The *Spaniards* borrowed these exercises from the *Moors*, and call them *juego de cannas*, reed or cane play. Some take them to be the same with *ludus Troganus*, anciently practiced by the your of *Rome*. The *Turks* use them still, and call them *lancing the gerid*.

The difference between *justs* and tournaments consists in this, that the latter is the genus, of which the former is only a species. Tournaments included all kinds of military sports and diversions made out of gallantry and diversion. *Justs* were those particular combats where the parties were near each other, and engaged with lance and sword : add that the tournament was frequently performed by a number of cavaliers who fought in a body. The *just* was a single combat of one man against another. Though the *just* was usually made in tournaments, after a general rencounter of all the cavaliers, yet they were sometimes singly, and independent of any tournament.

He who appeared for the first time at a just, forfeited his helm or casque, unless he had forfeited before at a tournament.

---

[1] Blaise de Vigenère (1523 – 1596), was a French diplomat, cryptographer, translator and alchemist.

The word is by some derived from the *French jouste*, of the *Latin juxta*, because the combatants fought near one another. *Salmasius*[1] derives it from the modern *Greek zoustr*a, or rather τζουστρα, which is used by *Nicephorus Gregoras*[2]. Others derive it from *justa*, which in the corrupt age of the *Latin* tongue was used for this exercise, by reason it was supposed a more just and equal combat than the tournament.

L

Gunners **LEVEL**, for leveling cannons and mortars, is an instrument consisting of a triangular brass plate about four inches high, at the bottom of which is a portion of a circle divided into 45°; which number is sufficient for the highest elevation, and for giving shot the greatest range. On the centre of this segment of a circle is screwed a piece of brass, by means whereof it may be fixed or moved at pleasure. The end of this piece of brass is made so, as to serve for a plummet and index, in order to shew the different degrees of elevation of pieces of artillery. This instrument has also a brass foot to set upon cannon or mortars, so as when those pieces are horizontal, the whole instrument will be perpendicular.

LIEUTENANT, *locum tenens*, a deputy, or officer, who holds the place of a superior, and discharges that function in his absence, which he ought to exercise in person. Of these, some are civil; as *lieutenants* of kingdoms, who are the kings viceroys, and govern in his stead; and lord *lieutenants* of countries. But the term is most frequent among military men, among whom there is a variety of *lieutenants*.

LIEUTENANT-*General*, a great officer, the next in rank to the general of an army; who, in battle, commands one of the lines or wings; a detachment in a march, or a flying camp. Also, a quarter at a siege, or one of the attacks, when it is his day of duty. In *France*, they have also *lieutenant-generals* of their naval forces who command immediately under the admirals. In

---

[1] Claude Saumaise (1588 - 1653), was a French classical scholar.
[2] Nikephoros Gregoras (ca. 1295 - 1360), was a Byzantine astronomer, historian and religious theologist.

Holland, they have a *lieutenant-admiral*, which is the same with what we call a *vice-admiral*.

LIEUTENANT-*General of the Ordnan*ce, is he who has charge of the artillery, batteries, &c. under the master general, or in his absence.

LIEUTENANT-*Colonel of Foot*, is the second officer in a regiment; he commands in the absence of the colonel, and in battle takes post at his colonel's left. The dragoons also have a *lieutenant-colonel*; but the horse have not, properly, any; the first captain of the regiment supplies the office.

LINE, in fortification, is sometimes take for a ditch, bordered with its parapet; and sometimes for a row of gabions, or sacks of earth, extended lengthwise on the ground, to serve as shelter against the enemy's fire. When the trenches were carried on within thirty paces of the glacis, they drew two *lines*, one on the right hand, the other on the left, for a place of arms.

LINE *of Defence*, is that which represents the course or flight of the bullet of any sort of fire-arms, more especially of a musket-ball, from the place where the musketeer must stand to scour and defend the face of the bastion.

LINE *of Defence fichant*, is that drawn from the angle of the curtin to that of the opposite bastion; without touching the face of the bastion. This must never exceed 800 feet, which they reckon the distance at which a musket-ball will do execution.

LINE *of Defence razant*, is that drawn from the point of the bastion along the face till it come to the curtin; and shows how much of the curtin will clear or scour the face. This is also called the *line of defence stringent*, or *flanking*.

LINE *of Approach*, or *Attack*, signifies the work the besiegers carry on under covert, to gain the moat, and the body of the place.

LINE *of Circumvallation*, is a *line* or trench cut by the besiegers, within cannon-shot of the place, which ranges round their camp, and secures its quarters against any relief to be brought the besieged.

LINE *of Contravallation*, is a ditch bordered with a parapet, which serves to cover the besiegers on the side of the place, and to stop the sallies of the garrison.

LINES *of Communication*, are those which run from one work to another. See *Tab. Fortif. fig.* 21. n. 2. 2. &c.

The **LINE** *of Communication*, is a continued trench, with which a circumvallation or contravallation is surrounded; and which maintains a communication with all its forts, redoubts, and tenailles.

LINE *of the Base*, is a right line which joins the points of the two nearest bastions.

LINE, in the art of war, is understood of the disposition of an army, raged in order of battle; with the front extended as far as may be, that it may not be flanked. An army usually consists of three *lines*; the first is the front, van, or advanced guard; the main body forms the second, in which is the general's post; the third is a reserved body, or rear guard. It is a rule to leave 150 paces distant between the first *line* and the second, and twice as much between the second and third, to give room for rallying.

LODGMENT, in military affairs, sometimes denotes an encampment made by an army.

LODGMENT is more frequently used for a work cast up by the besiegers, during their approaches, in some dangerous post, which they have gained, and where it is absolutely necessary to secure themselves against the enemies fire; as in a covert-way, in a breech, the bottom of a moat, or any other part gained from the besieged. *Lodgments* are made by casting up earth, or by gabions, or palisades, wool-packs, fascines, mantelets, or any thing capable of covering soldiers in the place where they have gained, and are determined to keep.

LUNETTE, in fortification, an enveloped counterguard, or elevation of earth, made in the middle of the foss, before the curtin, about five fathom in breadth. *Lunettes* are usually made in ditches full of water, and serve to the same purpose as fausse-brays, to dispute the passage of the ditch. The *lunette* consists of two faces, which form a re-entering angle; and its terreplein being only twelve feet wide, is a little raised above the level of the water; having a parapet three fathom thick.

M

MADRIER, in the military art, a thick plank, sometimes armed with iron plates, having a cavity sufficient to receive the mouth of a petard when charged; with which it is applied against a gate, or other body designed to be broke down.

MAGAZINE, in the military art, a place in fortified towns, where all sorts of stores are kept, and where carpenters, wheelwrights, smiths, &c. are employed in making things needful to furnish out the train of artillery.

MAJOR-*General*, is a general officer who receives the general's orders, and delivers them out to the *Majors* of brigades, with whom he concerts what troops are to mount the guard, what to go on parties, what to form detachments, or to be sent on convoys, &c. It is his business also to view the ground to encamp on, and do other services; being subordinated to the general, and lieutenant-general, and next commanding officer to them.

MAJOR *of a Brigade*, either horse or foot, is he who receives orders from the major-general, and gives them to the particular majors of each regiment,

MAJOR *of a Regiment*, is an officer whose business is to convey all orders to the regiment, to draw it up, and exercise it; to see it march in good order, and to rally if it be broke in an engagement, &c. The *Major* is the only officer of a regiment of foot, who is allowed to be on horseback in time of service; but he rides that he may speedily get from place to place, as occasion serves.

MANTELETS, in war, a kind of moveable parapet made of planks, about three inches thick, nailed on over another, to a height of almost six feet, generally cased with tin, and set upon little wheels; so that in a siege, they may be driven before the pioneers, to serve as blinds, to shelter them from the enemy's small shot. There are other sorts of *mantelets*, covered on the top, whereof the miners make use, to approach the walls of a town or castle. See *Tab. Fortif. fig.* 21.

It appears from *Vegetius*[1], that these were in use among the ancients, under the name of *vineae*; but they were built slighter, and larger than ours, being eight or nine feet high, as many broad, and sixteen long. They were defended

---

[1] Publius Flavius Vegetius Renatus (ca. 4th century), was a Roman author.

by a double covering, the one of boards, the other of faggots, with the ribs of osiers, and cased without with skins steeped in water to prevent fire.

MATROSSES, soldiers in the train of artillery, next below the gunners; their duty is to assist the gunners in traversing, sponging, loading, and firing of guns, &c. They carry fire-locks, and march along with the store wagons, both as a guard, and to help in case a wagon should break down.

MERLON, in fortification, that part of the parapet which lies betwixt two embrasures. It is usually from eight to nine feet long on the side of the cannon, and six on the side of the field; about six feet high and eighteen thick. The word comes from *merula*, or *merla*, which in the corrupt *Latin* was used for a battlement.

MILITIA, a collective term, understood of the body of soldiers, or persons who make profession of arms. The word comes from the *Latin miles*, a soldier; and *miles* from *mille*, which was anciently wrote *mile* : for in levying soldiers at *Rome*, as each tribe furnished a thousand, *mille* or *mile*, then, whoever was of that number, was called *miles*.

MILITIA, in its proper and restrained sense, is used to signify the inhabitants, or as we call them, the *trained-bands* of a town or country; who arm themselves on a short warning for their own defence. In which sense, *militia* is opposed to regular, stated forces.

The standing *militia* of *England* is now computed to be about 200000 horse and foot; but may be increased at the pleasure of the king. For the direction and command of these, the king constitutes *lords lieutenants* of each county, with power to arm, array, and form into companies, troops, and regiments, to conduct (upon rebellion and invasion) to employ the men so armed within their respective counties, and other places where the king commands; to give commissions to colonels, and other officers; to charge any person with horse, horse-man, arms, &c. proportionable to his estate.

No person to be charged with a horse unless he have 500 pounds yearly revenue, or 6000 pounds personal estate; nor with a foot-soldier, unless he have fifty pounds yearly, or 600 pounds personal estate.

MINE, in the art of war, denotes a subterranean canal, or passage dug under the wall, or rampart of a fortification, intended to be blown up by gunpowder. The *alley*, or passage of a *mine*, is usually about four foot square; at the end of this is the *chamber* of the *mine*, which is a cavity about five foot in width and in length, and about six in height; and here the gunpowder is bestowed. The *saucisse* of the *mine* is the train; for which there is always a little aperture made.

There are various kinds of *mines* which acquire various names; as royal *mines*, serpentine *mines*, forked *mines*, according as their passages are straight, winding, oblique, &c. There are also *mines* made in the field which are called *fougade*.

Mines are either dug within the body of the earth, as those made by the besieged to blow up the works of the besiegers, before they make a lodgment on the covered way : or in eminences and rising grounds, as to make a breech in the ramparts, &c. Or to blow up walls; or lastly to tear up rocks.

MINION, a sort of cannon, or piece of ordnance, whereof there are two kinds, large and ordinary.

The large **MINION**, or one of the largest size, has its bore 3¼ inch diameter, and is 1000 pounds weight; its load is 3½ pounds of powder; its shot three inches in diameter, and 3¼ pound weight; its length is eight foot, and its level range 125 paces.

The ordinary **MINION** is three inches diameter in the bore, and weighs about 800 pound weight. It is seven foot long, its load 2½ pounds or powder; its shot near three inches diameter, and weighs three pounds four ounces; and shoots point blank 120 paces.

MOAT, in fortification, a depth or trench dug around a town or fortress to be defended, on the outside of the wall or rampart. See *Tab. Fortif. fig.* 21. The depth and breadth of the *moat* often depend on the nature of the soil; according as it is marshy, rocky, or the like. The brink of the *moat* next the rampart in any fortification is called the *scarp*, and the opposite one the *counterscarp*.

Dry **MOAT** is that which is destitute of water; and ought to be deeper than the one which is full of water.

Lined **MOAT** is that whose scarp and counterscarp are cased with a wall of mason's work lying aslope.

MORTAR-PIECE, a short piece of ordnance, thick and wide, proper for throwing bombs, carcasses, shells, stones, &c. There are two kinds of mortars : the one hung or mounted on a carriage with low wheels, after the manner of guns; called *pendent*, or *hanging mortars*. The other fixed on an immovable base, called *standing mortars*.

At the head of the bore, or chase of the *mortar*, is the chamber for the charge of powder. This is usually made cylindrical, all but the base, which they make hemispherical : though some of the latter engineers prefer spherical chambers; as the surface of those being less, under equal capacities, make less resistance to the gunpowder.

The thickness of the *mortar* about the chamber is to be much greater than about the chase; by reason the gunpowder makes a much greater effort about the chamber than elsewhere : the diameter of the chamber to be much less than that of the bore; by reason bombs, shells, &c. are much lighter than the bullets of equal diameters; and, consequently, less powder suffices.

MUSKET, or **MUSQUET**, a fire-arm born on the shoulder, and used in war; to be fired by the application of a lighted match. The length of the *musket* is fixed at three feet eight inches from the muzzle to the touch-pan, and its bore is to be such as well receive a ball of sixteen in a pound. *Muskets* were anciently borne in the field by the infantry : at present they are little used save in the defence of places; fusees, or fire-locks having taken their place.

MUSKATOON, a *musket* shorter, though thicker than the ordinary *musket*. It is fired by the collision of steel and flint in the lock; whereas the *musket* is fired with a match. Its bore is a thirty-eighth part of its length; and carries five ounces of iron, with an equal quantity of powder.

MUSTER, a review of a body of forces under arms, in order to take account of the numbers, condition, accoutrement, arms, &c. The word is formed of the *French moustre*, specimen.

MUSTER-*master general*, or *commissary general of* MUSTERS, is an officer in the army who takes account of every regiment, their numbers, horses, arms, &c.

MUSTER-*rolls*, are list of the soldiers in every troop, company, regiment, &c. delivered by the captain to the commissary : by which they are paid, and the strength of the regiment known.

N

NAILING *of cannon*, the driving of a nail, or iron spike, by force, into the touch-hole of a piece of artillery; so as to render it for some time useless to the enemy.

OFFICERS *of war*, are those who have command in the forces. These are either *general, field*, or *subaltern officers*.

General **OFFICERS** are such whose command is not limited to a single troop, company, or regiment; but extends to a body of forces composed of several regiments. Such are the generals, lieutenant-generals, major-generals, and brigadiers.

Field **OFFICERS** are such as have command over a whole regiment; such are the colonel, lieutenant-colonel, and major.

Subaltern **OFFICERS** are the lieutenants, cornets, ensigns, sergeants, and colonels.

OPEN *Flank*, in fortification, is that part of the flank covered by the orillon.

ORDER, in war, denotes the arrangement of the parts of an army, either by land or sea; whether for marching, sailing, engaging, &c.

ORDER *of Battle*, is the placing the battalions and squadrons in one, two, or three lines, according as the ground will allow, either in order to engage the enemy, or to be reviewed by the general.

An **ORDER** *of March*, is disposed in two or three columns according to the ground. The *orders* and evolutions make the science of tactics.

ORDINANCE, or **ORDNANCE**, is also a general term for all great guns, or cannon, mortars, &c. The parts of a piece of *ordnance* are the outside, round about the piece, which is called the *superficies of her metal* : the substance, or whole mass of metal, called her *body* : the part next us, when she stands ready to fire, the *breech* or *coyle*; and the pummel, or the round knob at the end of it, the *cascabell*[1]; by some the *cascabell-dock*. The *trunnions* are the two knobs or ears which hold the piece in the carriage. *Maniglions* or *dolphins* in the *German* guns are two handles placed on the back of the piece near the trunnion, and near the centre of gravity, to mount and dismount them more easily

---

[1] A cascabel is a subassembly of a muzzle loading cannon; a place to attach arresting ropes to deal with the recoil of firing the cannon.

The rings about a piece of *ordnance* are five; the *base-ring*, that which is next below the touch-hole : the next above the touch-hole, is called the *reinforced-ring* : the next to that, forward, the *trunnion-ring* : the next to that, the *cornice-ring* : that at the mouth the *muzzle-ring* or the *freeze*. All the rings near the mouth are sometimes called the freezes.

As to the internal parts; the whole cavity or bore of the piece, is called her *chase* : that part of the cavity between the trunnions and the muzzle or the mouth, the *vacant cylinder* : that part of the trunnions to the end of the cavity, or so much of it as containeth (or is loaded with) the powder and shot, is called the *chamber*. The diameter of the mouth, the *caliber* : the space between the shot, and the hollow superficies of the piece within, the *vent*; being the difference between the diameter of the shot and the mouth of the piece.

Ordnance in *England* is distinguished into kinds, *viz. field-pieces* which are from the smallest to twelve pounds. And *cannon of battery* which are from culverin to a whole cannon.

Each of these divisions is again subdivided; the first into base, rabinet, falconet, falcon, minion ordinary, minion largest, saker least, saker ordinary, demi-culverin least, and demi-culverin ordinary. The second into culverin least, culverin ordinary, culverin largest, demi-cannon least, demi-cannon ordinary, demi-cannon large, and royal whole cannon.

The strength and serviceableness of a piece of *ordnance* depends much on the thickness of the metal, especially about its chamber and breech, which is called its *fortification*.

Of this there are three degrees both for cannon and culverins. Such as are ordinarily fortified are called *legitimate pieces*. Those whose fortification is lessened, are called *bastard pieces*. Those doubly fortified are called *extraordinary pieces*.

The fortification of a gun is reckoned from the thickness of the metal at the touch-hole, at the trunnions, and at the muzzle, in proportion to the diameter of the bore. The doubly fortified pieces are a full diameter of the bore at the touch-hole, 11/16 of it at the trunnions, and 7/16 at the muzzle : the lessened cannon have but 3/4 or 12/16 of the diameter of their bore, in the thickness at the touch-hole, 9/16 at the trunnions, and 5/16 at the muzzle.

All the double-fortified culverins, and all the lesser pieces of that kind, have a diameter 1/8 at the touch-hole, 15/16 at the trunnions, and 9/16 at the muzzle. And the ordinary fortified culverins are every way as the doubly fortified cannon; and the lessened culverins as the ordinary cannon, in all respects. The ordinary fortified cannon have 7/8 at the touch-hole, 5/8 at the trunnions, and 3/8 at the muzzle.

ORGUES, in the military art, thick long pieces of wood pointed and shod with iron, and hung each with a separate rope over the gateway of a city, ready on any surprize or attempt by the enemy to be let down to stop up the gate.

ORGUES is also used for a machine composed of several harquebuses or musquet-barrels bound together; by means whereof several explosions are made at the same time; used to defend breeches or other places attacked.

ORILLON, in fortification, a small rounding of earth, lined with a wall; raised on those bastions that have casemates; to cover the cannon in the retired flank, and prevent their being dismounted by the enemy. There are other sorts of *orillons*, properly called *epaulements*, almost of a square figure.

ORTEIL, in fortification. See *Berm*.

OUT-WORKS, in fortification. All those works made withoutside of the ditch of a fortified place, to cover and defend it. *Outworks*, called also *advanced* and *detached* works, are those which not only serve to cover the body of the place, but also to keep the enemy at a distance, and prevent his taking advantage of the cavities and elevations usually found in the places about the counterscarp; which might serve them either as lodgments, or as rideaux, to facilitate the carrying on their trenches, and planting their batteries against the place. Such are ravelins, tenailles, horn-works, queue d'arondes, envelopes, crown-works, &c.

The most useful of these are ravelins, or half-moons, formed between the two bastions, on the flanquant angle of the counterscarp, and before the curtin, to cover the gates and bridges.

ℙ

PALISADE, or **PALISADO**, in fortification, an inclosure of stakes or piles driven into the ground, six or seven inches square, and eight foot long; three of which are hidden underground. See *Tab. Fortif. fig.* 18. *Palisades* are used to fortify the avenues of open forts, gorges, half-moons, the bottom of ditches, the parapets of covert-ways; and in general in all posts liable to surprize, and to which the access is easy. *Palisadoes* are usually planted perpendicularly; though some make an angle inclining towards the ground next the enemy, that the ropes cast over them, to tear them up, may slip.

Turning **PALISADES**, are an invention of M. *Coehorn*, in order to preserve the palisades of the parapet of the covert-way from the besiegers shot. He orders them so, so that as many of them as stand in the length of a rod, or about ten foot, turn up and down like traps; so as not to be in sight of the enemy till they just bring on their attack : and yet are always ready to do the proper service of *palisades*.

PARAPET, *Breastwork*, in fortification, a defence or screen, on the extreme of a rampart or other work, serving to cover the soldiers and the cannon from the enemy's fire. *Parapets* are raised on all works where it is necessary to cover the men from the enemy's fire; both within and without the place, and even the approaches. Before the *Parapet* is a banquette, or little eminence, a foot and half high, for the soldiers to stand on.

The *Parapet Royal*, or that of the rampart, is to be of earth cannon proof, from 18 to 20 foot thick; six foot high towards the place, and four or five towards the rampart. This difference of height makes a glacis or slope for the musketeers to fire down into the ditch, or at least the counterscarp.

The *Parapet* of the wall is sometimes of stone. The *Parapet* of the trenches is either made of the earth dug up; or of gabions, fascines, barrels, sacks of earth, and the like.

PARK, in war. *Park of artillery*, a post in the camp out of shot of the enemy and fortified to secure the magazines and ammunition. Here are the artillery, artificial fireworks, powder, and other warlike provisions kept, and guarded by pikemen only, to avoid all casualties that might happen by fire. Every attack at a siege has its *park* of artillery.

PARTY, in the military sense, is used for a small body of men, whether cavalry, infantry, or both, commanded out on any expedition. By the *French*

military law, those who go out on *parties* should have an order in writing
from the commanding officer, and be at least twenty in number, if foot; or
twelve, if horse; otherwise they are reputed as robbers.

PATE, in fortification, a kind of platform, like what they call an horse-shoe;
not always regular, but usually oval, encompassed only with a parapet, and
having nothing to flank it. It is usually erected in marshy grounds, to cover
the gate of a town, or the like.

PELLICAN, is the name of an ancient piece of ordnance, carrying a ball of
six pounds; by the *French* made eight feet and a half, and by the *Dutch* nine
feet long.

PETARD, in war, a kind of engine of metal, somewhat in shape of a high-
crowned hat; serving to break down gates, barricades, draw-bridges, or the
like works which are intended to be surprized.

The *petard* may be considered as a piece of ordnance, very short, narrow at
the breach, and wide at the muzzle, made of copper mixed with a little brass,
or of lead with tin, usually about seven inches long, and five broad at the
mouth, weighing from forty to fifty pound.

Its charge is from five to six pounds of powder which reaches to within
three fingers of the mouth; the vacancy is filled with tow, and stopped with a
tampion; the mouth being very strongly bound up with cloth tied very tight
with ropes. It is covered up with a madrier or wooden plank that has a cavity
cut in it to receive the mouth of the *petard*, and fastened down with ropes
after the manner expressed in *Tab. Fortif. fig.* 5.

Its use is in a clandestine attack, to break down bridges, gates, barriers, &c.
to which it is hung; which it does by means of the wooden plank. It is also
used in countermines to break through the enemies galleries, and give vent to
their mines.

Some, instead of gun-powder for the charge, use one of the following
compositions, *viz.* gun-powder seven pounds, mercury sublimate one ounce,
camphor eight ounces; or gun-powder six pounds, mercury sublimate three
ounces, and sulphur three; or gun-powder six, beaten glass ½ ounce, and
camphor ¼;.

Petards are also sometimes made of wood bound round with iron hoops.

The invention of *petards* is ascribed to the *French Huguenots* in the year
1579; their most signal exploit was the taking of the city of *Cahors* by means
hereof, as we are told by *d'Aubigne[1]*.

PICKET, **PICQUET**, or **PIQUET**, in fortification, a stake sharp at one end,
and usually shod with iron; used in laying out the ground to mark the several

---

[1] Probably Théodore-Agrippa d'Aubigné (1552 – 1630), who was a French poet, soldier,
propagandist and chronicler.

measures and angles thereof. There are also larger *pickets* drove into the earth to hold together fascines or faggots in any work cast up in a haste.

PICKETS are also stakes drove into the ground by the tents of the horse, in a camp, to tie their horses to; and before the tents of the foot, where they rest their muskets or pikes about them in a ring.

PICQUEERING, PICKEERING, PICKEROONING, a little flying war, or skirmish, which the soldiers make when detached from their bodies, for pillage, or before a main battle begins.

PIECES, in the military art, include all sorts of great guns and mortars. These are also called pieces of ordnance or artillery.

Field **PIECES** are the smaller sort, carrying balls of ten or twelve pound.

Battery **PIECES** are the larger sort of guns used at sieges for making of breeches. Such are the twenty-four pounders and the culverin; the one carrying twenty-four, and the other eighteen pound of ball.

PIKE, an offensive weapon, consisting of a shaft of wood, twelve or fourteen foot long; headed with a flat pointed steel, called the *spear*. The *pike* was long time in use in the infantry to enable them to sustain the attack of the cavalry; but is now taken from them, and the bayonet, which screws on the end of the carabine, substituted in its place. Yet the *pike* still continues the weapon of foot-officers, who fight *pike* in hand, salute with the *pike*, &c. *Pliny* says the *Lacadaemonians* were the inventors of the *pike*. The *Macedonian* phalanx was a battalion of *pikemen*.

The name *pike* is said to be derived from a bird called by the *French pie*, by us wood-pecker, whose bill is so sharp as to pierce wood like an augre. *Du Cange* derives it from the base *Latin pica*, or pica, which *Turnebus*[1] supposes to have been so called, because resembling a kind of ear of corn; *Octavio Ferrari*[2] derives it *à spicula*. M. *Fauchet*[3] says, it is the *pike* gave name to the *Picards*, and *Picardy*, which he will have to be modern, and to have been framed on occasion of that people renewing the use of the pike, the etymology whereof he fetches from the *French piquer*, to prick : others will have the name *picard* to have been given that people by their readiness to pick quarrels, called in *French piques*.

---

[1] Adrien Turnèbe or Tournebeuf (1512 – 1565), who was a French classical scholar.
[2] Octavio Ferrari (1518 - 1586), who was professor of politics and ethics successively at Milan and Padua.
[3] Claude Fauchet (1530 – 1602), was a French historian and antiquary.

PLACE, in war, is a general name for all kinds of fortresses where a party may defend themselves. In which sense it may be defined to be a place so disposed as that the parts which encompass it defend and flank one another.

Strong, or *fortified* **PLACE**, is a *place* flanked and covered with bastions.

Regular **PLACE**, is that whose sides, angles, bastions, and other parts are equal; and is usually denominated from the number of its angles; as a pentagon, a hexagon, &c. *Palma nova*, built by the *Venetians*, is a dodecagon.

PLACE *of arms*, in fortification, is a strong city or town, pitched upon for the chief magazine of an army.

PLACE *of arms*, in a city or garrison, is a large open spot of ground, usually near the centre; where the grand guard is commonly kept, and the garrison holds its rendezvous at review, and in cases of alarm to receive orders from the governour.

PLACE *of arms*, of an attack, in a siege, is a spacious *place* covered from the enemy, by a parapet or epaulement, where the soldiers are posted ready to sustain those at work in the trenches, against the soldiers of the garrison.

PLACE *of arms particular*, in a garrison, is a *place* near every bastion, where the soldiers, sent from the grand *place* to the quarters assigned them, relieve those that are either upon the guard or in a fight.

PLACE *of arms without*, is a *place* allowed to the covert way, for the planting of cannon, to oblige those who advance in their approaches to retire.

PLATFORM, in war, an elevation of earth, on which cannon is placed to fire on the enemy. Such are the mounts on the middle of the curtins. On the rampart is always a *platform* where the cannon are mounted. It is made by heaping up of earth on the rampart, or by an arrangement of madriers, rising insensibly from the cannon to roll on; either in a casemate, or on an attack in the out-works.

PLATTOON, or **PLOTTOON**, in war, a small square body of 40 or 50 men, drawn out of a battalion of foot, and placed between the squadrons of horse to sustain them; or in ambuscades, streights, and defiles, where there is not room for whole battalions or regiments. The grenadiers are generally posted in *plattoons*.

To **POISON** *a piece*, among gunners, is the same as to clog and nail it up.

PONT *volant*, *flying bridge*, a kind of bridge used in sieges; made of two small bridges laid one over another, and so contrived by means of cords and pullies placed along the sides of the under-bridge, that the upper may be pushed forwards, till it join the place where it is designed to be fixed : the whole length of both not to be above five fathom, lest they should break with the weight of the men.

PORTCULLICE, in fortification, called also *herse* and *sarrasin*, an assemblage of several great pieces of wood laid or joined across one another like an harrow; and each pointed at the bottom with iron. The formerly used to be hung over the gate-ways of fortified places, to be ready to be let down in case of a surprize, when the enemy should come so quick as not to allow time to shut the gates. But now-a-days, the orgues are more generally used, as being found to answer the purpose better.

POST, in the military sense, is any spot of ground capable of lodging soldiers. A *post* denotes any ground or place, fortified or not, where a body of men may take a stand, and fortify themselves, or remain in a condition to fight the enemy. Hence they say, the *post* was relieved, the *post* was quitted, the *post* was taken sword in hand, &c.

A spot of ground seized by a party to secure the front of an army, and to cover the *posts* that are behind, is called an *advance post*.

The advanced guard, or the right of the two lines of an army, &c. are called the *post of honour*; and is always given to the oldest regiments.

The word is formed from the *Latin positus*, placed; some derive it from *potestas*, power.

POSTERN, in fortification, a small gate usually made in the angle of the flank of a bastion, or in that of the curtain, or near the orillon, descending into the ditch; whereby the garrison can march in and out, unperceived by the enemy, either to relieve the works, or make private sallies, &c.

PRIMING, or **PRIME** *of a Gun*, is the gun-powder put in the pan or touch-hole to give it fire. The priming is the last thing done in charging. For pieces of ordnance, they have a pointed iron rod, to pierce the cartridge thro' the touch-hole; called *primer*, or *priming-iron*.

Military **PYROTECHNY** is the doctrine of artificial fire-works and fire-arms, teaching the structure and use both of those used in war for the attacking fortifications, &c. as gun-powder, cannon, bombs, grenadoes, carcasses, mines, fusees, &c. and those made for amusement sake as rockets, stars, serpents, &c.

Some call *pyrotechny* by the name *artillery*; though that word is usually confined to the instruments of war. Others chuse to call it *pyrobology*, or rather *pyrobalogy*, *q.d.* the art of missile fires; from the *Greek* πυρ and βαλλειν, to cast, throw.

Wolfius[1] has reduced *pyrotechnia* into a kind of mathematical art : indeed it will not allow of geometrical demonstrations; but he brings it to tolerable rules and reasons : whereas before it had used to be treated by authors at random, and without regard to any reasons at all.

Q

QUADRANT, in gunnery, called also the *Gunner's Square*, is an instrument serving to elevate or point cannon, mortars, &c. according to the places they are to be leveled or directed to. It consists of two branches made of brass or wood; one about a foot long, eight lines broad, and one line in thickness; the other four inches long, and the same thickness and breadth as the former. Between these branches is a *quadrant* divided into 90 degrees, beginning from the shorter branch, and furnished with thread and plummet. See it figure in *Tab. Fortif. fig.* 4. Sometimes, also, on one of the surfaces of the long branch is noted the division of diameters and weights of iron bullets; as also the bores of pieces.

The use of this instrument is easy; nothing more being required but to place the longest branch in the mouth of the cannon or mortar, and elevate or lower it till the thread cuts the degree necessary to hit a proposed object.

QUADRILL, or **QUADRILLA**, a little troop or company of cavaliers, pompously dressed and mounted; for the performance of carousels, jousts, tournaments, runnings at the ring, and other gallant divertissements. A regular carousal is to have at least four, and at most twelve *Quadrills*. Of these *Quadrills*, each is to consist of at least three cavaliers, and at most twelve. The *Quadrills* are distinguished by the form of their habits, or the diversity of their colours.

The word is borrowed from the *Italian* being a derivative of *Squadra*, a company of soldiers arranged in a square : for *Squadrare* is, properly, to dispose any thing square; whence the *Quadriglia*, the *French Squadrille* and

[1] Christian Wolff (1679 – 1754), was a German philosopher.

Quadrille, and our *Quadrill*. It is not fifty years since the *French* wrote *Squadrille* and *Quadrille*.

QUARTER, in war, the place allotted to certain forces to live, lodge, and encamp upon, during a siege, or the like. The general's *Quarter* is that where the general lodges and incamps in person. They used to make lines of communication to join the several *Quarters* together.

QUARTER is also used for any lodgment made in the field or campaign out of a siege. Thus they say, the general has extended his *Quarters* a good way. The enemy coming by made him contract his quarters.

QUARTER *of assembly*, is the place of rendezvous where the troops are to meet and draw up to march in a body.

QUARTER also denotes the safety and good treatment promised to persons, or troops that surrender, and lay down their arms. Thus they say, the enemy begged *Quarter*. The phrase took its rise from an agreement anciently made between the *Dutch* and *Spaniards*, that the ransom of an officer or soldier, should be a quarter of his pay. Hence, to beg *Quarter* was to offer a *Quarter* of their pay for their safety; and to refuse *Quarter* was not to accept that composition for their ransom.

QUARTER-WHEELING, or **QUARTER** *of conversion*, in the military art, is the motion whereby the front of a body of men turned round to where the flank was; this making a quarter of a circle. If it be done to the right, the man in the right hand angle keeps his ground and faces about, while the rest wheel; if to the left, the left hand man keeps his place, &c.

QUEUE D'ARONDE, in fortification, *q.d.* Swallow-tail, a term applied to out-works, when narrower at the gorge than the face or front; *i.e.* where the sides open towards the campaign and contract towards the gorge. The name is occasioned by its resemblance to a swallow's tail, which the *French* call *queue d'aronde*. Of this kind are some single as well as double tenailles; and some horn-works whose sides are not parallel. On the contrary, when the sides are less than the gorge the work is called *contre queue d'aronde*.

ℜ

RAMMER *of a gun*, or *gun-stick*; a rod or staff used in charging a gun, to drive home the powder to the breech, as also the shot, and the wad, which keeps the shot from rolling out.

RAMPART, or **RAMPIER**, in fortification, a massy bank or elevation of earth raised about the body of a place, to cover it from the great shot; and formed into bastions, curtins, &c. See *Tab. Fortif. fig.* 21. *lit. rr.* The word is formed from the *Spanish amparo*, defence, covering.

Upon the *rampart* the soldiers continually keep guard and pieces of artillery are planted for the defence of the place. Hence, to shelter the guard from the enemy's shot, the outside of the *rampart* is built higher than inside, *i.e.* a parapet is raised upon it with a platform. Hence, also, earth, not being able to be raised perpendicularly like stone; the rampart is built with a talus or slope, both on the inner and outer side.

The *rampart* is sometimes lined, *i.e.* fortified with a stone wall within side, otherwise it has a berme. It is incompassed with a moat or ditch, out of which the earth that forms the *rampart* is dug.

The height of the *rampart* should not exceed three fathom; this being sufficient to cover the houses from the battery of the cannon : neither ought its thickness to be above 10 or 12, unless more earth be taken out of the ditch, than can be otherwise bestowed.

The *ramparts* of half-moons are the better for being low; that the small fire of the defendants may the better reach the bottom of the ditch : but yet they must be so high as to not be commanded by the covert-way.

RANGE, in gunnery, the path of the bullet, or the line it describes from the mouth of the piece to the point where it lodges. If the piece be laid in a line parallel to the horizon it is called the *right* or *level range*. If it be mounted to 45 degrees the ball is said to have the *utmost range*; and so proportionally, all others between 0 degrees and 45 degrees being called the *intermediate ranges*.

RANGING, in war, the disposing of troops in a condition proper for engagement or for marching. The army was *ranged* in form of battle to receive the enemy; ranged in three columns for a march, &c. In building, the side of a work that runs straight without breaking into angles is said to *range*, or *run range*.

RANK, in military discipline, denotes a series or row of soldiers placed side by side; a number of which *ranks* for the depth of the squadron or battalion, as a number of files does the width. To *close the rank* is to bring the men nearer : to open, to set them further apart. To *double the ranks* is to throw two into the space of one, by which the files are thinned.

RASANT, or **RAZANT**, in fortification. *Rasant flank* or *line* is that part of the curtin, or flank, whence the shot exploded raze or glance along the face of the opposite bastion. The defence of the bastion is *rasant*.

RATION, or **RATIAN**, in the army, a pittance, or proportion of ammunition, bread, drink, or forage, distributed to each soldier for his daily subsistence. Some write the word *racion*, and borrow it from the *Spanish racim*. But they both come from the *Latin ratio* : in some parts of the sea they call it *reason*. The horse have *rations* of hay and oats when they cannot go out to forage. The *rations* of bread are regulated by weight. The ordinary *ration* of a foot soldier is a pound and half of bread per day. The officers have several *rations* according to their quality and the number of attendants they are required to keep. When the *ration* is augmented on account of rejoicing, it is called *double ration*.

RAVELIN, in fortification was anciently a flat bastion placed in the middle of a curtin.

RAVELIN is now a detached work, composed only of two faces, which make a salient angle without any flanks; and raised before the curtin on the counterscarp of the place. A *ravelin* is a triangular work resembling the point of a bastion with the flanks cut off. See *Tab. Herald. fig.* 21. Its use before the curtin is to cover the opposite flanks of the next two bastions. It is used also to cover a bridge or a gate; and is always placed without the moat. What the engineers call a *ravelin*, the soldiers generally call a *demi-lune*, or half-moon. There are also *double-ravelins* which serve to defend each other. They are said to be double when they are joined by a curtin.

REBUS, a name-device, as *Cambden* Englishes it; or an enigmatical representation of some name, &c. by using a figure, or picture, instead of a word, or part of a word. Such is that of the gallant, mentioned by *Cambden*, who expresses his love to *Rose Hill*, by painting in the border of his gown, a rose, a hill, an eye, a loaf, and a well; which in the *rebus*-style, reads, *rose hill I love well*.

The *Picards* have the honour of the invention of this notable kind of wit; whence the French, to this day, call it, *rebus de Picardie*. Camden adds, that the *English* first learned it of them in the reign of our *Henry* III by means of the garrisons we then had in *Calais*, *Guinne*, and other places bordering on *Picardy*.

It's origin is by *Menage*, &c. ascribed to the priests of *Picardy*, who, it seems, anciently, in carnival-time, used every year to make certain libels entitled, *de rebus quae gerunteur*, being railleries on what intrigues and transactions had passed about the city; wherein, they made great use of such sort of equivoques and allusions, breaking and joining words, and supplying them with paintings. Thus in the rebus of *Picardy*, says *Marot*; a curry-comb, *etrille*; a scythe, *faux*; and a calf, *veau*, make *etrille fauxveau*. But the practice has since been prohibited by reason of the scandal.

Cambden tells us, the rebus was in wonderful esteem among our fore-fathers; and that he was nobody who would not hammer out of his name an invention by this wit-craft, and picture it accordingly.

The sieur *Des Accords*[1], has made an ample collection of the most famous *rebus's de Picardy*. And Mr. *Cambden* has done something of the same kind in his Remains. The abbot of *Ramsey*, he tells us, engraved in his seal a ram in the sea, with this verse, to shew he was a right ram, *cujus signa gero, dux gregis est ut ego*[2]. Sir *Thomas Caval* (Caval signifying a horse) engraved a galloping horse in his seal, with this limping verse, *Thomae Creditis, cum cermitis ejus equum*[3]. So *John Eagleshead* bore in his seal an eagle's head, with this motto around it, *Hoc aquilae caput est, signumque figura Johannis*[4].

Bolton[5], prior of St. *Bartholomew's*, signified his name by a bolt thrust through a tun. *Islip*, abbot of *Westminster*, a man highly in favour with *Henry* VII had a quadruple *rebus* for his single name; sometimes he set up in his windows the figure of an eye with a slip of a tree; sometimes the letter I with the said slip; in other places one slipping boughs in a tree; and in others, one slipping from a tree; with the word, I-slip.

Thomas, earl of *Arundel*, signified his name by a capital A in a rundle. *Morton*[6], the great archbishop of *Canterbury*, was content to use mor upon a tun; and sometimes a mulberry called morus, out of a tun. So *Luton*, *Thornton*, *Ashton*, &c. signified their names by a lute, a thorn, an ash, upon a tun. So a hare on a bottle was the device of *Harebottle*; a mag-pye on a goat, of *Pigot*; a hare by a sheaf of rye in the sun, of *Harrison*; *Lionel Ducket*[7] used a lion with an L on its head, whereas says *Cambden*, it should have been on its tail : had the lion been eating a duck, adds the same author, it had been a

---

[1] Probably Étienne Tabourot, seigneur des Accords(1549 - 1590), who was a French jurist, writer and poet.
[2] He, whose sign I bear, is leader of the flock, as I am.
[3] Trust in Thomas when you see his horse.
[4] This is the head of an eagle, the seal and badge of John.
[5] William Bolton (ca. 1450 - 1532), was prior of St. Bartholomew's and clerk of works for Westminster Abbey.
[6] John Morton (c. 1420 – 1500), was an English prelate who served as Archbishop of Canterbury from 1486 to 1500.
[7] Lionel Duckett (1511 – August 1587), was a wealthy merchant and Lord Mayor of London in 1572.

rare device, worth a ducat or a duck-egg. *Garret Dews* signified his name on his sign by two men in a garret casting dews at dice.

Abel Drugger's device in *Ben Johnson's Alchymist*, and *Jack of Newbury* in the spectator, are known to every body. But the *rebus* being once raised to sign posts, grew out of fashion at court, and has been left to hang there ever since; indeed attempts have been lately made for its rescue by a reverend divine, in his *Tunbridge-Love-Letters*, &c.

Yet has the *rebus* antiquity on its side, as havibg been in use in the pure *Augustan* age : *Cicero*, in a dedication to the Gods, inscribe *Marcus Tullius*, with a little pea, called by the *Latins cicer*, by us as chick-pea. And *Julius Caesar*, in some of his coins, used an elephant, called *Caesar* in the *Mauritanian* tongue. Add to these, that the two mint masters in that age, *L. Aquilius Florus*, and *Voconius Vitulus*, used, the first a flower, the second a calf, on the reverse of their coins.

REDOUBT, REDOUTE, REDUCTUS, in fortification, a small square fort, without any defence but in front; used in trenches, lines of circumvallation, contravallation, and approach; as also for the lodging of corps de garde, and to defend passages. The word is *French*, formed from the *Latin reductus*.

In marshy grounds, *redoubts* are often made of stone-work for the security of the neighbourhood : their face consists of from ten to fifteen fathom; the ditch around them from eight to nine foot broad and deep; and their parapets have the same thickness.

REGIMENT, in war, a body consisting of several troops of horse, or companies of foot, commanded by a colonel. The number of men in a *regiment*, is as undetermined as that of the men in a troop or company.

There are *regiments* of horse that are not above 300 men; and there are some in *Germany* of 2000; and the regiment of *Picardy* in *France* consists of 120 companies, or 6000 men. The *French regiments* of horse are not commanded by a colonel as the foot are, but by a mestre de camp.

Some observe that were no *regiments* of horse before 1637. Till then the troops were loose and independent of each other, not incorporated into a body or *regiment*.

RETIRADE, in fortification, a kind of retrenchment made in the body of a bastion, or other work, which is to be disputed inch by inch, after the first defences are dismantled. It usually consist of two faces which make a re-entering angle. When a breech is made in a bastion, the enemy may also make a *retirade*, or a new fortification behind it.

RETIRED *Flank*, in fortification. See *Flank*.

RETREAT, in war, the retiring, or moving back again of an army, or part thereof. We say, to sound a *retreat*, secure a *retreat*, &c. What they call a *retreat* in the armies, is really a flight; only a flight made by design, and with conduct. The skill and ability of the general is known by his *retreats*, more than his engagements. The *retreat* of the ten thousand *Greeks* under the command of *Xenophon* has been admired in all antiquity.

RETRENCHMENT, in war, denotes any kind of work thrown up to strengthen or defend a post against an enemy. Such are ditches with parapets, gabions, fascines, &c. for a covering, &c. The enemy came with design to oblige them to raise the siege, but could not force the retrenchments.

RETRENCHMENT is more particularly used for a simple retirade made on a horn-work, or bastion; when it is intended to dispute the ground inch by inch. It is usually a reentering angle whose faces flank each other; and fortified with ditches, parapets, gabions, &c.

REVEILLE, a beat of the drum in the morning, intended to give notice that it is day-break; and that the soldiers are to rise, and the sentries forebear challenging.

RHINE-LAND-*Rod*, in fortification, a measure of two fathom, or twelve foot, used by the Dutch and German engineers, &c.

RIDEAU, in fortification, a small elevation of earth, extending itself lengthways on a plain; serving to cover a camp or give advantage to a post. The *rideau* is also convenient for those who would besiege a place at a near distance, and to secure the workmen in their approaches to the foot of a fortress. The word in its original *French* signifies a curtain or cover; formed from the *Latin ridellum. Borel* [1] derives it from *ridere*.

RIDEAU, is also sometimes used for a trench, the earth whereof is thrown up on its side; to serve as a parapet for covering the men.

*Muster-***ROLL**, that wherein are entered the soldiers of every troop, company, regiment, &c. As soon as a soldier's name is wrote down on the roll, it is death for him to desert.

RONDEL, in fortification, a round tower sometimes erected at the foot of a bastion.

ROUL, ROLL, or **ROWL**, in the military art. Officers of the same rank, who mount the same guards, and take their turns in relieving one another, are said to *roul* or *roll*.

---

[1] Possibly Pierre Borel, or Petrus Borellius (ca. 1620 – 1671), whowas a French doctor of medicine, a chemist and botanist, and was physician to Louis XIV.

ROUND, is a military term, signifying a walk or turn which an officer, attended with some soldiers, takes in a garrison or fortified place, *around* the ramparts, in the night-time; to listen of any thing be stirring without the works, and to see that the sentries are watchful, do their duty, and all things in good order.

In strict garrison, the *rounds* go every quarter of an hour, that the rampart may always be furnished. The sentries are to challenge at a distance; and to rest their arms as the *rounds* pass, and let no one come near them.

When the *round* is near the corps de garde, the sentry calls aloud, *who comes there?* and when the answers is, *the rounds*, he says, *stand*; then calls for the corporal of the guard, who draws his sword, and calls also, *who comes there?* and when it is answered, *the rounds*, he that has the word advances and delivers it to the corporal, who receives it with his sword pointed at the giver's breast.

ROYAL *army*, is army marching with heavy cannon, capable of besieging a strong, well fortified city. It is usual to hang up a governour, who has the assurance to hold out a petty place against a royal army.

ROYAL *parapet*, or *parapet of the rampart*, in fortification, is a bank about three fathoms broad, and six foot high, placed upon the brink of the rampart, towards the country; to cover those who defend the rampart.

𝕾

SAIGNER, in fortification, a *French* term, signifying to bleed or drain. Hence, *saigner la fosse*, is to empty of drain the water out of the moat, by conveyances underground; that it may be passed over the more easily, by laying hurdles or rushes on the mud remaining.

SAKER, a sort of small cannon whereof there are three species : *extra-ordinary*, *ordinary*, and *least sized*.

SAKER *Extraordinary*, is about four inches diameter at the bore, 1800 pound weight, and ten foot long; its load five pounds, shot three inches and a half diameter, and something more than seven pound and a quarter weight; its level range is 163 paces.

SAKER *Ordinary*, is a size less, three inches three quarters size bore, nine foot long, 1500 weight; its charge four pounds of powder, bullet's diameter three inches and a half, weight six pounds, its level range1 60 paces.

SAKER *of the least Size*, is three inches and a half diameter at the bore, 1400 pound weight, eight foot long, its load near three pounds and a half; shot four pounds three quarters weight, and three inches and a quarter diameter.

SALET, **SALLET**, or **SALADE**, in war, a light covering, or armour for the head, anciently wore by the light horse; only differing from the cask, in that it had no crest, and was little more than a bare cap. *Nicod*[1] derives the word from *Sila*, which had the same significance among the *Latins* : others from *Saladinus*, alledging that it was borrowed from the orientals; others from the *Italian Celeta*, as if the head was hid hereby. Others from the *Spanish Celada*, a little cask.

SALIENT, in fortification, denotes projecting.   There are two kinds of angles; the one *Saliant*, which are those that present their points outwards. The other *Re-entering*, which have their points inwards. Instances of both kinds we have in tenailles and star-works.   The word is formed from the *French Saillant*, which signifies the same thing; of *sailler*, to project, advance outwards, and that of the *Latin salire*, to leap.

---

[1] Probably Jean Nicot de Villemain (1530 — ca. 1600), who was a French diplomat and scholar.

SALLY, in the military art, the issuing out of the besieged from their town or fort, and falling upon the besiegers to cut them off, nail their cannon, hinder the progress of their approaches, destroy their works, &c. We say to make a *Sally*, to repulse a *Sally*, &c.

SAND-BAGS, in fortification, are bags holding each about a cubic foot of earth or sand; used for raising parapets in haste, or to repair what is beaten down. They are also of use when the ground is rocky, and affords not earth to carry on the approaches; because they can be easily brought on and off at pleasure. There are a lesser sort which hold half what the former do, and are placed upon the upper talus of the parapet, to cover those who are behind, and who fire through the embrasures, or intervals, that are between them.

SAP, in the military work, denotes a work carried on underground, to gain the descent of a ditch, counterscarp, or the like. It is performed by digging a deep trench, descending by steps from top to bottom, under a corridor; carrying it as far as the bottom of the ditch, when that is dry, or the surface of the water when wet.

When the covert way is well defended by musketeers, the besiegers make their way down into it by *sapping*. See *Tab. Fortif. fig.* 21. n. 5. When they are got near the foot of the glacis, the trench is carried on directly forwards; the workmen covering themselves with blinds, wool-packs, sand-bags, and mantelets upon wheels. They also make epaulements, or traverses, on each side, to lodge a good body of men.

The *sap* is usually made five or six fathom from the salient angle of the glacis, where the men are only covered side-ways; for which reason they lay planks over head with hurdles, and earth above them.

When they have forced the enemy to quit the covert-way, the pioneers immediately with sand-bags, wool packs, or other fences, make a lodgment and cover themselves as well as they can, from the fire of the opposite bastion.

SARRASIN, or **SARRAZIN**, in fortification, a kind of portcullice otherwise called an *herse*, which is hung with ropes over the gate of the town, or fortress, and let fall in case of surprize.

SAUCISSE, SAUSAGE, in the military art, a long train of powder sewed up in a roll of pitched cloth, about two inches in diameter; serving to set fire to mines or caissons. The length of the *saucisse* is to extend from the chamber of the mine, to the place where the engineer stands to spring the mine. There are usually two *saucisse* to every mine; that if the one should fail, the other may take effect.

SAUCISSON, in fortification, a kind of faggot made of the thick branches of trees, or of the trunks of shrubs bound together : whose use is to cover the men, and to serve as epaulements. The word is *French* and signifies literally a big sausage. The *saucisson* differs from a *fascine*, which is only made of the small branches, and by its being bound at both ends, and in the middle.

Anciently, they made the *saucisson* 46 foot long and 15 foot thick; since it is 23 foot long, and 12 thick; bound strongly together with three bands strengthened with iron.

SCALADO, or **SCALADE**, a furious assault made on the wall or rampart of a city, by means of ladders where with to mount without carrying on works in form to secure the men. Cities are now no longer taken by *scalade* since the walls have been flanked.

SCARP, in fortification, the interior slope of the ditch of a place; that is, the slope of that side of the ditch which is next to the place, and faces the campaign. The *scarp* commences from the liziere or foot of the rampart. The *scarp* is opposite to the counterscarp which is the other side of the ditch.

SCONCES, small forts, built for the defence of some pass, river, or other place. Some *sconces* are made regular, of four, five, or six bastions; others are of smaller dimensions, fit for passes, or rivers; and others for the field. The profiles (that is, the thickness and height of the breastworks) to be set on these several works, and the ditches, are to be accommodated to the occasion. Such are,

1. Triangles with half bastions; which may be all of equal sides. However it be, divided the sides of the triangle into three equal parts, one of these three parts will set off the capitals and gorges; and the flanks, being at right angles to the side, make half of the gorge;
2. Square with half bastions; whose sides may be between 100 and 200 feet, and let one third of the side set off the capitals and the gorges, but the flank (which raise at right angles to the sides) must be but one half of the gorge or capital, that is, on the sixth part of the side of the square.
3. Square with half bastions, and long.
4. Long squares.
5. Star redoubt of four points.
6. Star redoubt of five or six points.
7. Plain redoubts, which are either small or great. The small are fit for court of guards in the trenches, and may be squares of 20 feet to 30. The middle sorts of redoubts may have their sides from 30 to 50 feet; the great ones from 60 to 80 feet square.

SENTINEL, CENTINEL, or **SENTRY**, in war, a private soldier taken out of a corps de garde of foot, and placed on some post to watch any approach of the enemy, to prevent surprizes; and to stop such as would pass without orders, or without discovering who they are. The *sentinel's* word when he challenges is, *Who is there? Qui vive*, or *Qua va la? Stand! Demeure la!*

Sentinel perdu is a *sentinel* placed at some very advanced and dangerous place, whence it is odds he never returns.

The word is modern; it is not long since they said *To be on the scout*, in the same sense as we now say, *To stand sentry*, &c.

SERGEANT, or **SERJEANT**, in war, is an inferior officer in a company of foot, or troop of dragoons; armed with halbard, and appointed to see discipline observed, to teach the soldiers the exercise of their arms, to see due distances kept, to order, straighten, form ranks, files, &c.

SIEGE, in war, the encampment of an army around place, with design to take it, either in the way of distress and famine, by making lines all around it, to prevent any relief from without; or by main force, as by digging trenches, and making formal attacks. The word is *French*, and literally signifies *seat*; alluding to the army's taking its seat here till the reduction of the place. The most celebrated *sieges* of antiquity, are *Troy, Tyre, Alexandria, Numantium,* &c. Among the moderns, those of *Ostend, Candia, Grave*, &c.

SILLON, in fortification, an elevation of earth made in the middle of the moat, to fortify it when too broad. The *sillon* is more usually denominated *envelope*.

SIXAIN, **SIXTH**, **SEXAGENA**, in war, an ancient order of battle, whereas six battalions being ranged in one line, the second and fifth are made to advance, to form the vanguard; the first and sixth to retire, to form the rear guard; and the third and fourth remaining on the spot to form the corps, or body of the battle.

SKIRMISH, in war, a disorderly kind of combat, or encounter, in presence of two armies between small parties, or persons who advance from the body for that purpose, and introduce, or invite to a general regular fight.

The word seems formed from the *French escarmouche*, which signifies the same, and which *Nicod* derives from the *Greek* χαρμη, which signifies at the same time both light, combat and joy : *Menage*[1] derives it from the *German schirmen* or *skirmen*, to fence or defend : *Du Cange* from *scaramuccia*, a light engagement, of *scara* and *muccia*, a body of soldiers hid in ambush; in regard most *skirmishes* are performed by persons in ambuscade.

SOLDIER, a military man, listed to serve a prince or state, in consideration of a certain daily pay. The *soldier* is he who takes pay; the vassal he who is obliged to serve at his own expences; the volunteer he who serves at his own

---

[1] Gilles Ménage (1613 – 1692), was a French scholar.

expence, and of his own accord. *Du Cange* observes, that the ancient *soldiers* were not to be short of five foot and a half; and that this measure was called *incoma*, or *incomma*.

The word is formed from the *Italian soldato*, and that from the *Latin solida* or *solidata*, of *solidus*, the solde, or pay; though *Pasquier*[1] chuses to derive it from the old *Gaulish souldoyer*, a soldier; and *Nicod* from *soldurius*.

SPAHI, **SIPAHI**, horsemen in the *Ottoman* army, chiefly raised in *Asia*. The great strength of the grand Signior's army consists in the janizaries who are the foot, and the *spahi's*, who are the horse.

SPUNGE, is used in gunnery, for a long staff or rammer, with a piece of sheep or lamp-skin wound about its end, to serve for scouring great guns when discharged, before they are charged with fresh powder.

SPUNGING, in gunnery, the clearing a gun's inside with a *spunge*, in order to prevent any sparks of fire remaining in her, which would endanger the life of him who should load her again.

SQUADRON, a body of horse, whose number of men is not fixed, but is usually from one hundred to two hundred. The word is formed from the *Italian squadrone*, of the *Latin squadro*, used by corruption for *quadro* : in regard, at first, the *squadrons* were always square, and called also by the *Latins agmina quadrata*.

The *squadron* usually consists of three troops; and each troop of fifty men : it never exceeds two hundred, because a greater number cannot be advantageously posted, nor have room to act in narrow grounds, woods, marshes, defiles, &c. A *squadron* is always drawn up three deep, or in three ranks, with the length of an horse between each rank. The standard is always bore in the centre of the first rank. The eldest troop takes the right of the *squadron*, and the second the left, the youngest being in the centre.

SQUARE *Battle*, or *battalion* of men, is one that hath an equal number of men in rank and file. To form any number of men into a square battle, as suppose 500, extract the nearest square root of 500, which is in integers 22, and what will give the number of men for rank and file. There will be a remainder of 16 men, who may be disposed of, as the commander thinks best.

Hollow **SQUARE**, in the military art, is a body of foot drawn up with an empty space in the middle, for the colours, drums and baggage; faced and covered by the pikes every way to keep off horse.

---

[1] Étienne Pasquier (1529 – 1615), was a French lawyer and author.

STANDARD, in war, a sort of banner or flags, bore as a signal for the joining together of the several troops belonging to the same body. The *standard* is usually a piece of silk, a foot and a half square, on which is embroidered the arms, device, or cypher of the prince, or the colonel. It is fixed on a lance, eight or nine foot long, and carried in the centre of the first rank of a squadron of horse.

The *standard* is used for any martial ensign of horse; but more particularly for that of the general; or the royal *standard*. Those bore by the foot are rather called *colours*.

The ancient kings of *France* bore St. *Martin's* hood for their *standard*. The *Turks* preserve a green *standard* born by *Mahomet*, with a world of devotion; as believing it to have been brought down by the angel *Gabriel*. Every time it is displayed, all who profess the *Mahometan* faith, are obliged to take arms; those who refuse are to be deemed as infidels.

Du Cange derives the word from *standarum* or *stantarum*, *standardam*, or *standale*, words used in corrupt *Latin*, to signify the principal flag of an army. *Menage* derives it from the *German stander*, or the *English stand*.

STAR, in fortification, a little fort with five or more points, or salient and re-entering angles, flanking one another, and their faces 90 or 100 foot long. Formerly, *star* forts were frequently made in lines of circumvallation, after two or three redoubts.

STRAPADO, or **STRAPPADO**, a kind of military punishment, wherein the criminal's hand being tied behind, he is hoisted up by a rope, to the top of a long piece of wood, and let fall again almost to the ground; so that by the weight of his body in the shock, his arms are dislocated. Sometimes he is to undergo three *strapados* or more.

The word is formed from the *French estrapade* which signifies the same; and which is supposed to have come from an old proverb *estreper*, to break, extirpate; or from the *Italian strappata*, of the verb *strappare*, to wrest by force.

SUBALTERN, a subordinate officer, or one who discharges his post under the command and direction of another. Such are lieutenants, sub-lieutenants, cornets and ensigns, who serve under the captain. The word is formed from the *Latin sub*, and *alter*, another.

SUSPENSION *of arms*, in war, is a short truce which the contending parties agree on, for the burial of their dead, the waiting for succours, or the order of their masters, &c.

SWALLOW-TAIL, in fortification, a kind of out-work only differing from a single tenaille, in that its sides are not parallel as those of the tenaille, but narrower towards the fortified place, than towards the country.

T

TACTICKS, the art of disposing forces in battle, and of performing the military motions and evolutions. The word is *Greek* τακτικα, from ταξις, order. The *Greeks* were very skillful in this part of the military art, having public professors of it, called *Tactici*, who taught and instructed their youth therein. *Aelian[1]* hath a particular book on this subject; and there is a great deal of it in *Arrian[2]* in his history of *Alex. M.[3]* and in *Mauritius*, and *Leo Imperator[4]*. *Vossius[5], de scient. Mathmat.* mentions 24 ancient authors on the subject of *Tacticks*.

TAIL *of the trenches*, in the military art, is the post of place where the besiegers begin to break ground, to cover themselves from the fire of the town. The *Tail* of the trench is the first work which the besiegers make at the opening of the trenches; as the head of the attack is that carried on toward the place.

TALUS, in fortification. *Talus of a Bastion*, or *Rampart*, is the slope or diminution allowed to such a work; whether it be of earth or stone; the better to support its weight. The *exterior Talus* of a work is its slope on the side towards the country; which is always made as little as possible, to prevent the enemies scalade; unless the earth be bad, and then it is absolutely necessary to allow a considerable *Talus* for its parapet. The *interior Talus* of a work, is its slope on the inside toward the place.

TAMPION, TOMPION, TAMKIN, or **TOMKIN**, a kind of plug or stopple serving to close a vessel; particularly to keep down the powder in a fire-arm. The word is formed from the *French tampon*, a bung, stopple, &c. Some derive it from the *English tap*.

In charging a mortar, or the like, over the powder is usually put a thin round piece of wood to keep the shot, ball, shell, or the like, from the gun-powder. This piece is called a *Tampion*, and by means hereof the shot is exploded with the greater vehemence.

---

[1] Aelianus Tacticus (ca. second century AD), was a Greek military writer.
[2] Arrian of Nicomedia, or Lucius Flavius Arrianus Xenophon (ca. AD 86 – ca. 160), was a Roman (born in Greece) historian, public servant, military commander and philosopher.
[3] Refers to Arrian's book "The Anabasis of Alexander" and his campaign in Macedonia.
[4] Flavius Valerius Leo (401 – 474), known in English as Leo the Thracian or Leo I, was a Byzantine emperor who ruled from 457 to 474.
[5] Gerrit Janszoon Vos (1577 – 1649), was a Dutch classical scholar and theologian.

TAPER-BORED, is applied to a piece of ordnance, when it is wider at the mouth than towards the breech.

TAT-TOO, *q.d. Tap to*, a beat of a drum at night, to advertise the soldiers to retreat, or repair to their quarters in a garrison, or to their tents in a camp.

TENABLE, in the military art, something that may be defended, kept, and held against assailants. The word is *French*, formed from *tenir*; as that from the *Latin tenere*, to hold. *Tenable* is little used but with a negative; when a place is open on all sides, and its defences all beaten down, it is no longer *tenable*. When the enemy has gained such an eminence, this post is not *tenable*.

TENAILLE, in fortification, a kind of out-work consisting of two parallel sides, with a front, wherein is a re-entering angle. In strictness, that angle, and the faces which compose it, are the *tenaille*. The *tenaille* is of two kinds; *simple*, and *double*.

Simple, or *single* **TENAILLE**, is a large out-work, such as DABCE, consisting of two faces or sides, AB and CB, including a re-entering angle B. See *Tab. Fortif. fig.* 6. & 21.

Double, or *flanked* **TENAILLE**, is a large out-work consisting of two simple *tenailles*, or three saliants, and two re-entering angles, FGH and HIK. See *Tab. Fortif. fig.* 7. & 21. The great defects of *tenailles* are, that they take up too much room, and on account are advantageous to the enemy; that the angle B is undefended; the height of the parapet hindering seeing down into it, so that the enemy can lodge there under covert; and that the sides AD and CE are not sufficiently flanked. For these reasons, *tenailles* are not excluded out of fortifications by the best engineers; and never made, but where there wants time to form a horn-work.

TENAILLE *of the Place*, is the front of the place, comprehended between the points of two neighbouring bastions; including the curtin, the two flanks raised on the curtin, and the two sides of the bastions which face one another. So that the *tenaille* is the same with what is otherwise called the *face of a fortress*.

TENAILLE *of the Ditch*, is a low work raised before the curtin in the middle of the foss or ditch. It is of three sorts : the first is composed of a curtin, two flanks, and two faces : the rampart of the curtin, including the parapet and talus, is but five fathom thick, but the rampart of the flanks and faces seven. See *Tab. Fortif. fig.* 21.

The second, which *Vaubin*[1] saith he found to be of very good defence, is composed only of two faces, made on the lines of defence, whose rampart and faces are parallel.

The third sort only differs from the second in this, that its rampart is parallel to the curtin of the place.

All three sorts are good defences for the ditch, and lie so low, that they cannot be hurt by the besiegers cannon, till they are masters of the covert-way, and have planted their artillery there.

TERRE-PLEIN, in fortification, the top platform, or horizontal surface of the rampart where the cannon are placed, and the defenders perform their office. It is thus called, as lying level, having only a single slope outwardly to bear the recoil of the cannon. It is terminated by the parapet on that side towards the campaign, and by the inner talus on the side towards the place. Its breadth is from 24 to 30 feet.

TERTIATE, in gunnery. To *tertiate* a great gun, is to examine the thickness of the metal at the muzzle, whereby to judge of the strength of the piece, and whether it be sufficiently fortified or not. This is usually done with a pair of caliper compasses, and if the piece be home-bored, the diameter less by the height, divided by two, is the thickness at any place.

TESTUDO, *Tortoise*, in the military art, was a kind of cover or screen which the soldiers, *q.d.* a whole company, made themselves of their bucklers, by holding them up over their heads, and standing close to each other. This expedient served to shelter them from darts, stones, &c. thrown down upon them, especially those thrown from above when they went to the assault.

TESTUDO, was also a kind of large wooden tower which moved on several wheels, and was covered with bullocks hides flayed, serving to shelter the soldiers when they approached the walls to mine them or batter them with rams.

TRAIN is used for a line of gun-powder laid to give fire to a quantity thereof, in order to do execution, by blowing up earth, works, buildings, &c.

TRAVERSE, in gunnery, signifies to turn or point a piece of ordnance which way one pleases upon her platform. The laying or removing a piece of ordnance or a great gun, in order to bring it to bear, or lie level with the mark, is also called *traversing the piece.*

---

[1] Sébastien Le Prestre de Vauban, Seigneur de Vauban and Marquis de Vauban (1633 – 1707), was a French military engineer and Marshall of France.

TRAVERSE, in fortification, denotes a trench, with a little parapet, sometimes two, one on each side, to serve as a cover from the enemy that might come in flank. *Traverses* are sometimes covered over with planks and loaded with earth. They are very commodious for stopping an enemy's way, and to prevent being enfiladed. They likewise make a good defence in a dry foss, in making the parapet on the side next the opposite flank.

TRAVERSE, in a wet foss, is a sort of gallery, made by throwing saucissons, joysts, fascines, stones, earth, and other things into the foss, over against the place where the mine is to be put to the foot of the wall, in order to fill up the ditch, and make a passage over it.

TRAVERSE also denotes a wall of earth or stone raised across a work which is commanded, to cover the men.

TRAVERSE also signifies any retrenchment, or line fortified with fascines, barrels or bags of earth, or gabions.

TRENCHES, in fortification, are ditches the besiegers cut to approach more securely to the place attacked; whence they are also called *lines of approach*. See *Tab. Fortif. fig.* 21. They say, *mount the trenches*, that is, go upon duty in them. To *relieve the trenches*, is to relieve such as have been upon duty there. The enemy is said to have *cleared the trenches*, when they have driven away if killed the soldiers who guarded them.

Tail of the **TRENCH**, is the place where it was begun. And the *head*, that to which it was carried. *Trenches* are of several sorts according to the nature of the soil : if the adjacent territory be rocky, the *trench* is only an elevation of bavins, gabions, wool-packs, or epaulements of earth, cast round about the place – but where the ground may be easily opened, the *trench* is dug therein, and bordered with a parapet on the side of the besieged. The breadth of the *trenches* is from eight to ten foot, and the depth from six to seven, they are cut in talus, or a-slope.

   The *trenches* are to be carried on with winding lines, in some manner parallel to the works of the fortress, so as not to be in view of the enemy, nor to expose their length to the enemy's shot : for then they will be in danger of being enfiladed, or scoured by the enemy's cannon : this carrying of the *trenches* obliquely, they call carrying them by *coudees*, or returns.

Opening the **TRENCHES**, is when the besiegers begin to work upon the lines of approaches, which is usually done in the night; sometimes within musket-shot, and sometimes within half or whole cannon-shot of the place, if there be no rising ground about it, the garrison strong, and their cannon well served.

The workmen that open the *trenches* are always supported by bodies of men against the sallies of the besieged; and sometimes those bodies lie between them and the place, as also on their right and left. The pioneers sometimes work on their knees; and the men that are to support them lie flat on their faces in order to avoid the enemy's shot; and the pioneers are likewise usually covered with mantelets or saucissons.

TROOP, a small company of horse or dragoons, numbering about 50; commanded by a captain : answering to a company of foot.

To beat the **TROOP**, is the same with beating the assembly.

TRUCKS, among gunners, round pieces of wood in form of wheels, fixed on the axle-trees of carriages; to move the ordnance at sea, and sometimes on land.

TRUNNIONS, or **TRUNIONS**, of a piece of ordnance, those knobs or bunches of the gun's metal, which bear her up on the cheeks of the carriage.

TRUNNION *ring*, is the ring about the cannon next the *trunnions*.

TURNAMENT, or **TOURNAMENT**, a martial sport or exercise, which the ancient cavaliers used to perform, to shew their bravery, and address.

The first *turnaments* were only courses on horseback, wherein the cavaliers tilted at each other with canes, in manner of lances; and were distinguished from jousts, which were courses or careers, accompanied with attacks and combats with blunted lances and swords. Others say, it was a *turnament* when there was only one quadril or troop; and that where there were several to encounter each other, it was a joust. But it is certain the two became confounded together in process of time.

The prince who published the *turnament*, used to send a king at arms with a safe conduct, and a sword to all the princes, knights, &c. signifying that he intended a *turnament* and a clashing of swords, in the presence of ladies and damsels; which was the usual formula of invitation.

They first engaged man against man, then troop against troop; and after the combat, the judges allotted the prize to the best cavalier, and the best striker of swords; who was, accordingly, conducted in pomp to the lady of the *turnament*; where after thanking her very reverently, he saluted, and likewise her two maids.

These *turnaments* make the principle diversions of the XIIIth and XIVth centuries. *Munster*[1] says, it was *Henry the Fowler*[2], duke of *Saxony*, and afterwards emperor, that first introduced them; but it appears from the

---

[1] Probably Sebastian Münster (1488 – 1552), who was a German cartographer, cosmographer, and a scholar.
[2] Henry the Fowler (876 – 936), who was the Duke of Saxony and the King of Germany.

chronicle of *Tours*, that the true inventor of this famous sport, was one *Geoffrey[1]*, lord or *Preuilli*, about the year 1066.

From *France* they passed into *England* and *Germany*. The *Historia Byzantina* tells us, that the *Greeks* and *Latins* borrowed the use thereof from the *Franks*; and we find mention made of them in *Cantacuzenus[2]*, *Gregorius*, *Bassarion[3]*, and others of the late *Greek* authors.

Budaeus[4] derives the word from *trojana agmina*; others from t*rojamentum, quasi ludus trojae*. *Menage* deduces it from the *Latin tornensis*, or the *French tourner*, in regards the combatants turned and twisted this way and that. M. *Paris[5]* calls them in *Latin hastiludia*; *Neubrigensis[6]*, *meditationes militares*; others *gladiaturae*, others *decursiones ludicri*, &c.

Pope *Eugenius* II excommunicated those who went to *turnaments*, and forbad them burial on holy ground. K. *Henry* II of *France* died of a wound received at a *turnament*. One *Chiaoux*, who had assisted at a tournament under *Charles* VIII, said very happily, *If it be in earnest, it be too little; if in jest, too much.*

It is to the exercise of *turnaments*, we owe the first use of armories; of which the name blazonry, the form of the escutcheons, the colours, principle figures, &c. are undeniable evidences. Those who had not been in any *turnaments*, had no arms, though they were gentlemen.

In *Germany* it was anciently a custom to hold a solemn *turnament* every three years, to serve as proof of nobility. For the gentleman who had assisted at two, was sufficiently blazoned and published, *i.e.* he was acknowledged noble, and bore two trumpets by way of crest on his *turnament* cask.

TURNPIKE, is used in the military art, for a beam stuck full of spikes, to be placed in a gap, a breech, or at the entrance to a camp, to keep off the enemy.

The *turnpike*, called also *cheval de frise*, is a spar of timber twelve or fourteen foot long, and about six inches diameter; of a sexangular form, bored with holes, one right under another, about an inch in diameter; the axis of the holes being six inches from one another, and to go in from each side. Those intended to be thrown into breeches must be made of oak; and need not be so big, or the pickets so long.

The spikes or pickets which are driven into the holes, are five or six feet long, pointed with iron; and with wedges or nails fastened tight into the

---

[1] Godfrey de Preuilly, (? - 1066), was a French knight credited with writing the rules for the sport of jousting.
[2] John VI, Kantakouzenos or Cantacuzenus (ca. 1292 – 1383), was the Byzantine emperor and afterwards pursued literary works.
[3] Basilios, or Basilius, Bessarion (1403 – 1472), was a Roman Catholic Cardinal Bishop and the Latin Patriarch of Constantinople, and a Greek scholar and author.
[4] Guillaume Budé (1467 – 1540), was a French scholar.
[5] Possibly Matthew Paris (ac. 1200 – 1259), who was a Benedictine monk, English chronicler, artist in illuminated manuscripts and cartographer.
[6] William of Newburgh or Newbury (ca. 1136 – ca. 1198), also known as William Parvus, was an English historian and Augustinian canon.

holes. Two of these fastened together with an iron chain and staple, six inches long, are of great use to stop the enemy in the breeches or elsewhere.

VAN-COURIERS, are light armed soldiers, sent before to beat the road, upon the approach of an enemy.

VAN-FOSSE, a ditch dug without the counterscarp, and running all along the glacis; usually full of water.

VAN, or **VAN-GUARD**, is a military term, signifying the first line of an army drawn up in battalia. It is the same with the *front* of an army, and gives the first charge upon the enemy. Every army is composed of three parts, a *van-guard*, a *rear-guard*, and the *main body*.

VEDETTE, in the military art, a sentinel on horseback, detached from the main body of the army, to discover and give notice of the enemy's designs.

WAR, *Bellum*, a contest or difference between princes, states, or large bodies of people; which not being determinable by the ordinary measures of justice and equity, is referred to the decision of the sword. *Hobbes's*[1] great principal is, that the natural state of man is a state of warfare; most other politicians hold war to be a preternatural and extraordinary state.

Civil, or *Intestine* **WAR**, is that between subjects of the same realm; or between parties in the same state. In this sense we say, the *civil wars* of the *Romans* destroyed the republic; the *civil wars* of *Grenada* ruined the power of the *Moors* in *Spain*; the civil wars in *England* begun in 1641 ended in the king's death, 1648.

King's **WAR**, *Bellum regis*. At the time when particular lords were allowed to make *war* with one another, to revenge injuries, instead of prosecuting them in the ordinary courts of justice; the appellation *king's war* was given to such as the king declared against any other prince or state : on which occasion, the lords were not allowed to make private *war* against each other; being obliged to server the king with all their vassals, &c.

Religious **WAR**, is a *war* maintained in a state on account of religion; one of the parties refusing to tolerate the other.

Holy **WAR**, is that anciently maintained by leagues and croisades for the recovery of the holy land.

WATCH, *Guet*, a person posted as a spy in any place, to have an eye thereto, and give notice of what passes.

WATCH, is also used for a *corps de garde* posted at any passage; or a company of guards who go on patrol. Some officers are exempted from *watch* and guard. In the same sense they say, *night-watch*, guet de nuit; *watch-word*, mot de guet; *royal-watch*, *city-watch*. *Chevalier de guet*, is a name given by the *French*, to the officer who commands the *royal-watch*, &c.

---

[1] Thomas Hobbes of Malmesbury (1588 – 1679), was an English philosopher.

WINGS, *alae*, in the military art, are the two flanks, or extremes of an army, ranged inform of battle; being the right and left sides thereof, and including the main body. The cavalry are always posted in the *wings*, *i.e.* on the flanks, or the right and left sides of each line, to cover the foot in the middle.

This, at least, is certain, that the method of arranging in *wings* is very ancient. The *Romans*, we know, used the term *alae*, or *wings*, for two bodies of men in their army; one on the right, the other on the left, consisting each of 400 horse, and 4200 foot usually, and wholly made up of confederate troops. These were designed to cover the *Roman* army as the *wings* of a bird cover its body. The troops in these *wings*, they called *alares*, and *alares copiae*; and we at this day distinguish our armies into the *main body*, the *right* and *left wings*.

WINGS, in fortification, denote the longer sides of horn-works, crown-works, tenailles, and the like outworks; including the ramparts and parapets, with which they are bounded on the right and left, from the gorge to their front. These wings, or sides, are capable of being flanked, either with the body of the place, if they stand not too far distant, or with certain redoubts; or with a traverse made in their ditch.

WORD, *Watch-***WORD**, in an army, or garrison, is some peculiar word, or sentence, by which the soldiers know, and distinguish one another in the night, &c. and by which spies and designing persons are discovered. It is used also to prevent surprizes. The *word* is given out in an army every night by the general to the lieutenant or major-general of the day, who gives it to the majors of the brigades, who give it to the adjutants; who give it first to the field-officers, and afterwards to a sergeant of each company, who carry it to the subalterns. In garrisons it is given, after the gate has shut, to the town-mayor who gives it to the adjutants, and they to the sergeants.

WORKS, *Opera*, in fortification, the several lines, trenches, ditches, &c. made round a place, an army, or the like, to fortify and defend it.

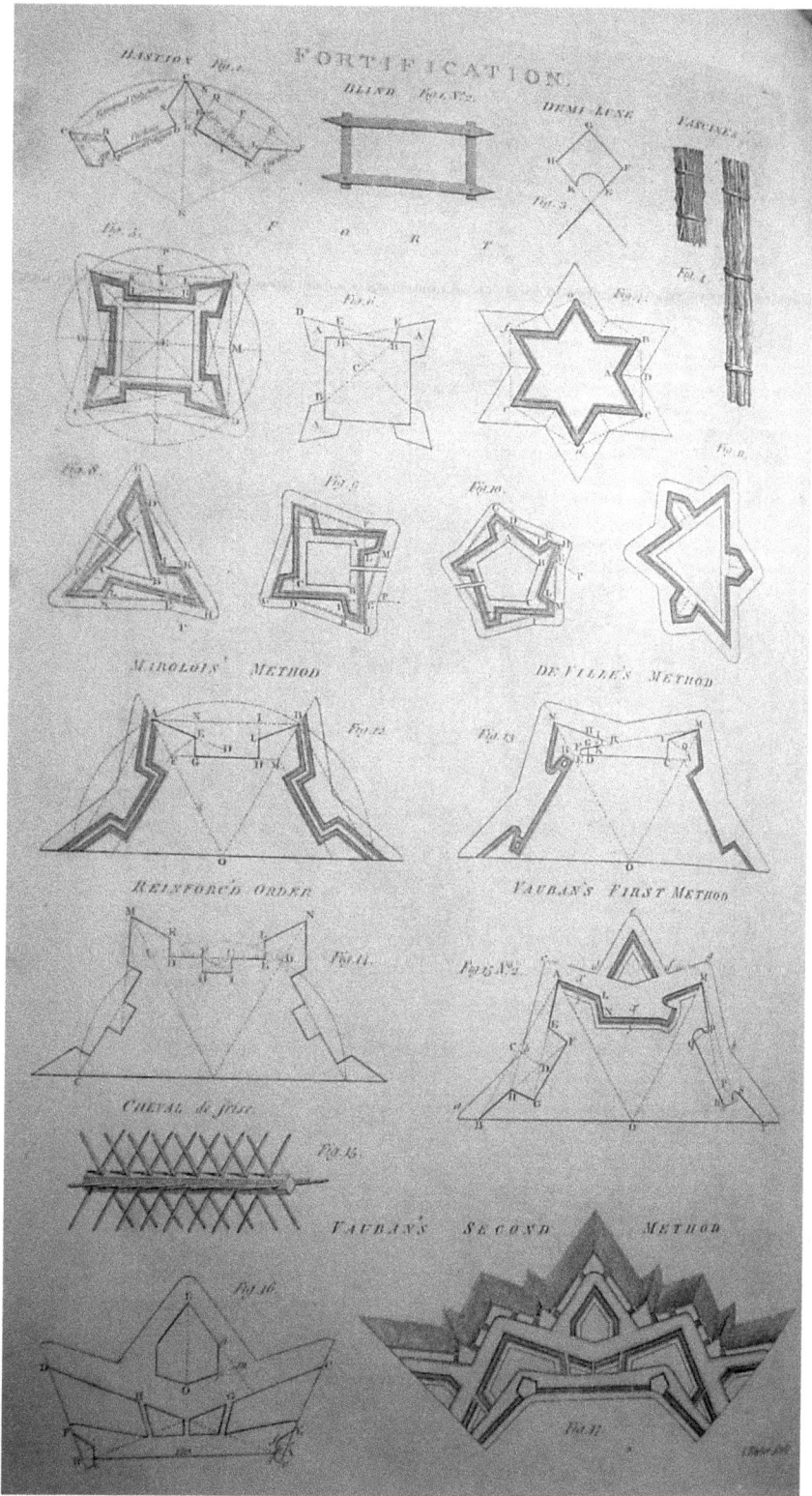

FORTIFICATION.

FORTIFICATION *Tab. II.*

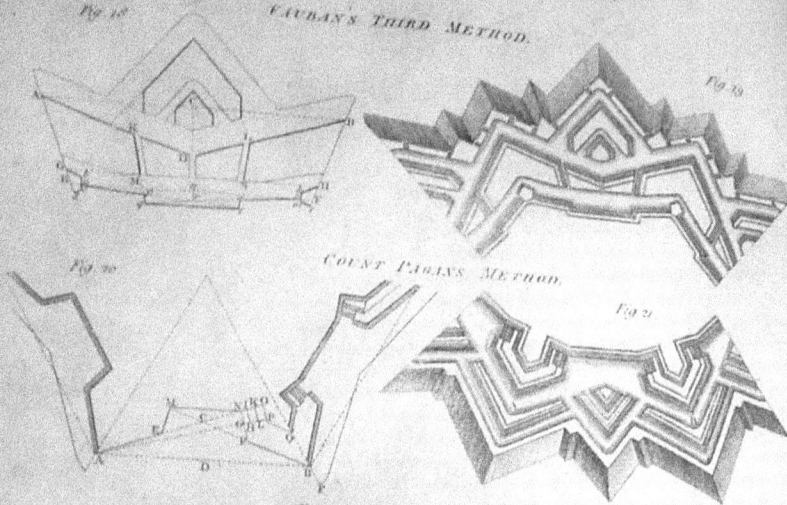

Fig. 18 VAUBAN'S THIRD METHOD.

Fig. 19

COUNT PAGANS METHOD.

Fig. 20 *Fig. 21*

FORTIFIED *Place*

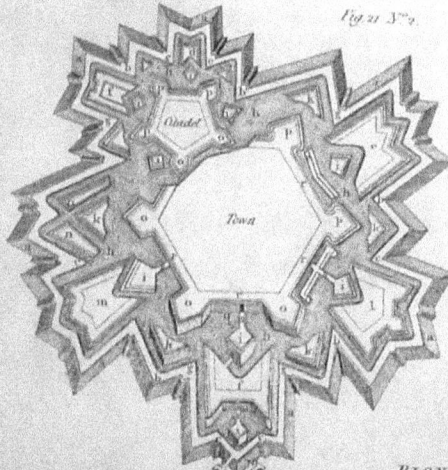

Fig. 21 N°2.

NAMES of the WORKS.

a. *Glacis or Dalerie*
b. *Covert way*
c. *Counterscarp*
d. *Single Tenaille*
e. *Double Tenaille*
o. *Tenaille in the Ditch*
f. *Horn Work*
g. *Places of Arms*
h. *The Moat or Ditch*
i. *Ravelin*
k. *Half Moon*
l. *Crown Work*
m. *Bonnet or Priests Cap*
n. *Counter Guard*
o. *Bastion*
p. *Bastions with Circular Flanks*
q. *Curtain*
r. *Rampart or Wall*
s. *Bridge*

NAMES of the APPROACHES.

1. *Trenches of approach*
2. *Lines of Communication*
3. *Batteries*
4. *Forts for Defence of the Trenches*
5. *a Sap*
6. *a Mine*

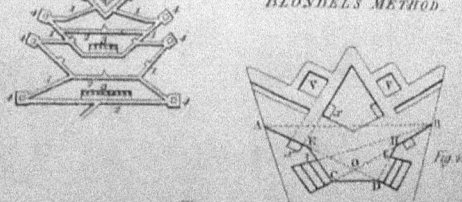

BLONDELS METHOD.

Fig. 22

BATTERY *Fig. 23 N°1*

Fig. 23

FORTIFICATION. *Tab. III*

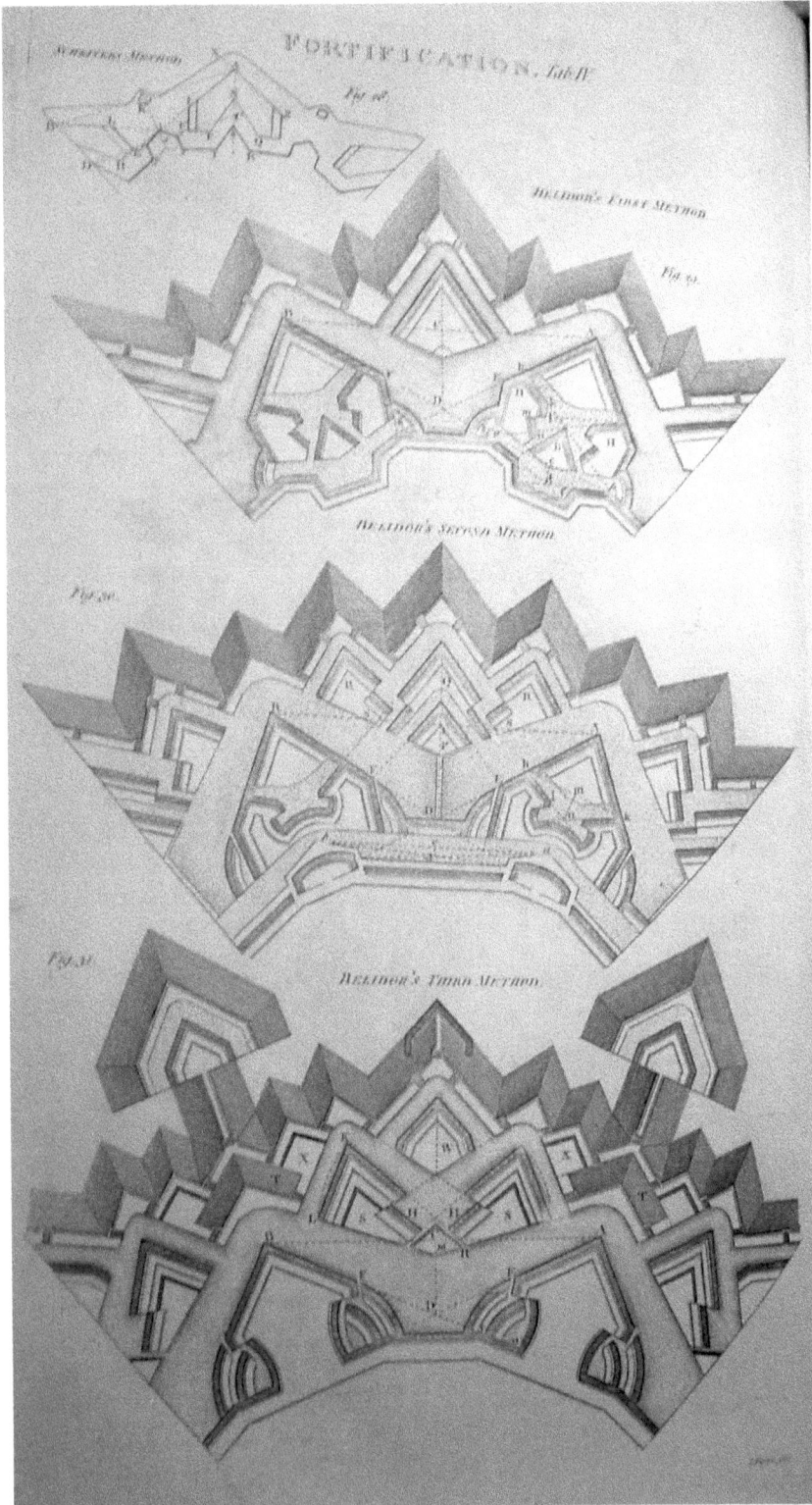

FORTIFICATION, *Tab.IV.*

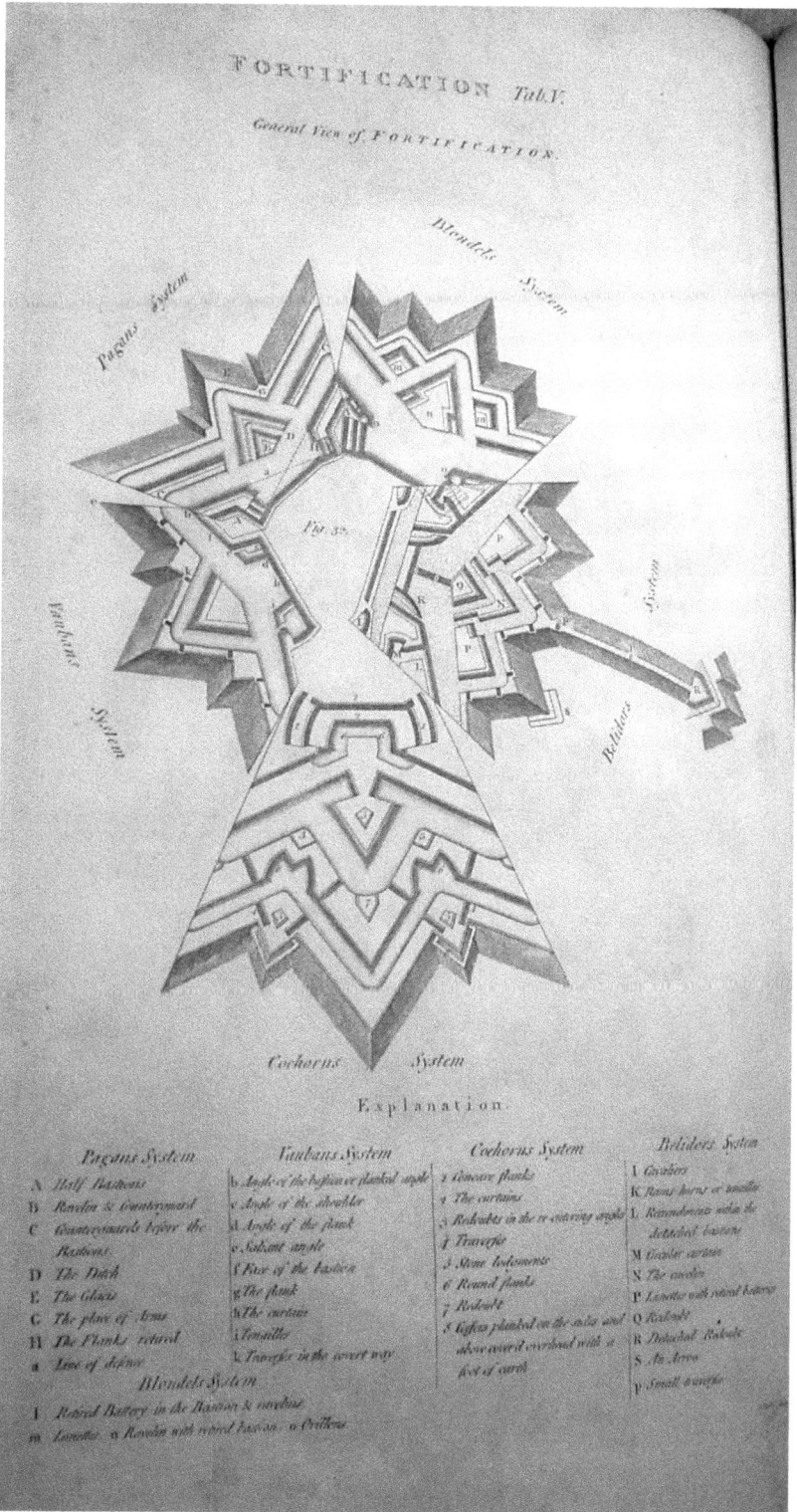

FORTIFICATION Tab. V.

General View of FORTIFICATION

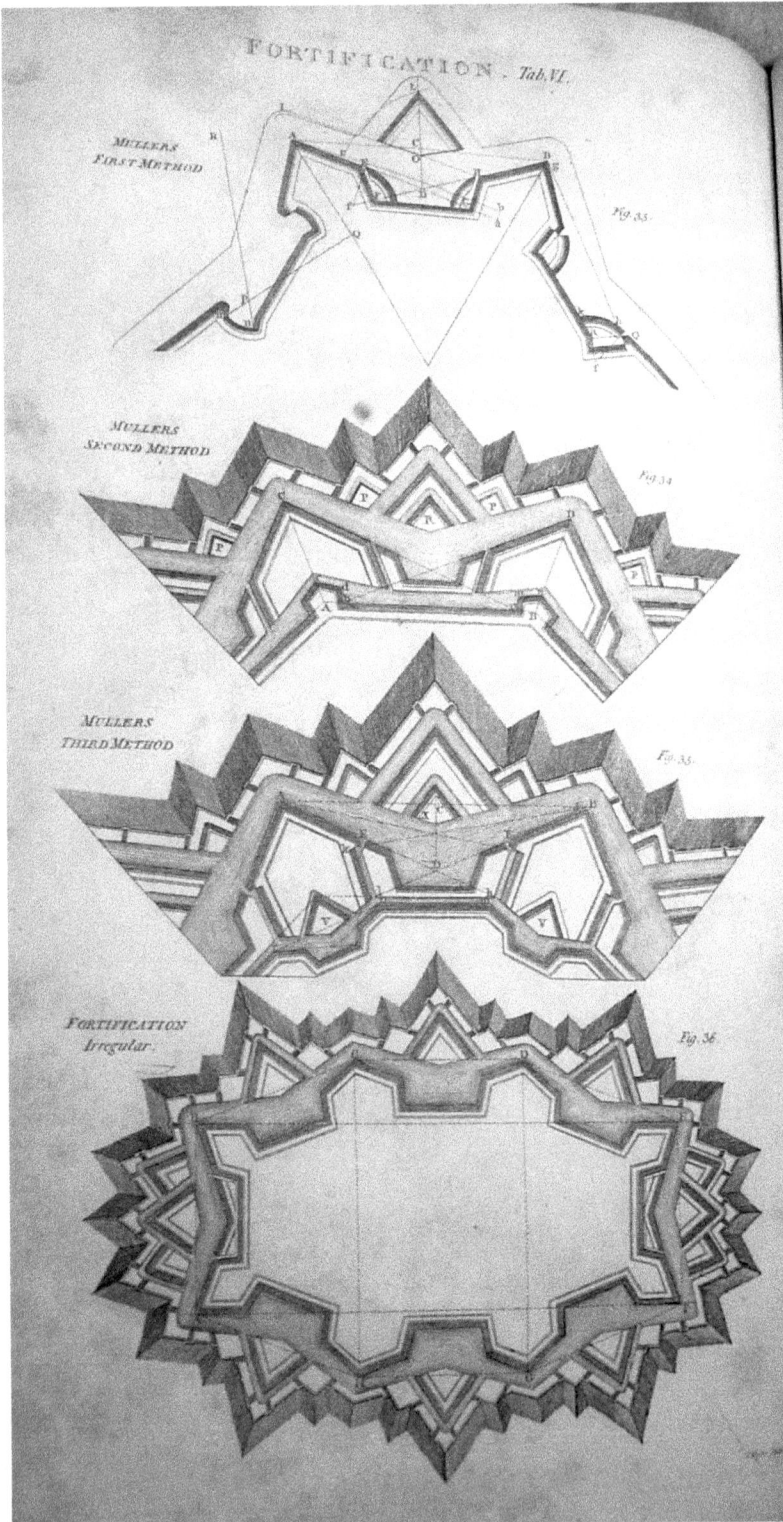

FORTIFICATION. Tab.VI.

MULLERS
FIRST METHOD

Fig.33.

MULLERS
SECOND METHOD

Fig.34.

MULLERS
THIRD METHOD

Fig.35.

FORTIFICATION
Irregular.

Fig.36.

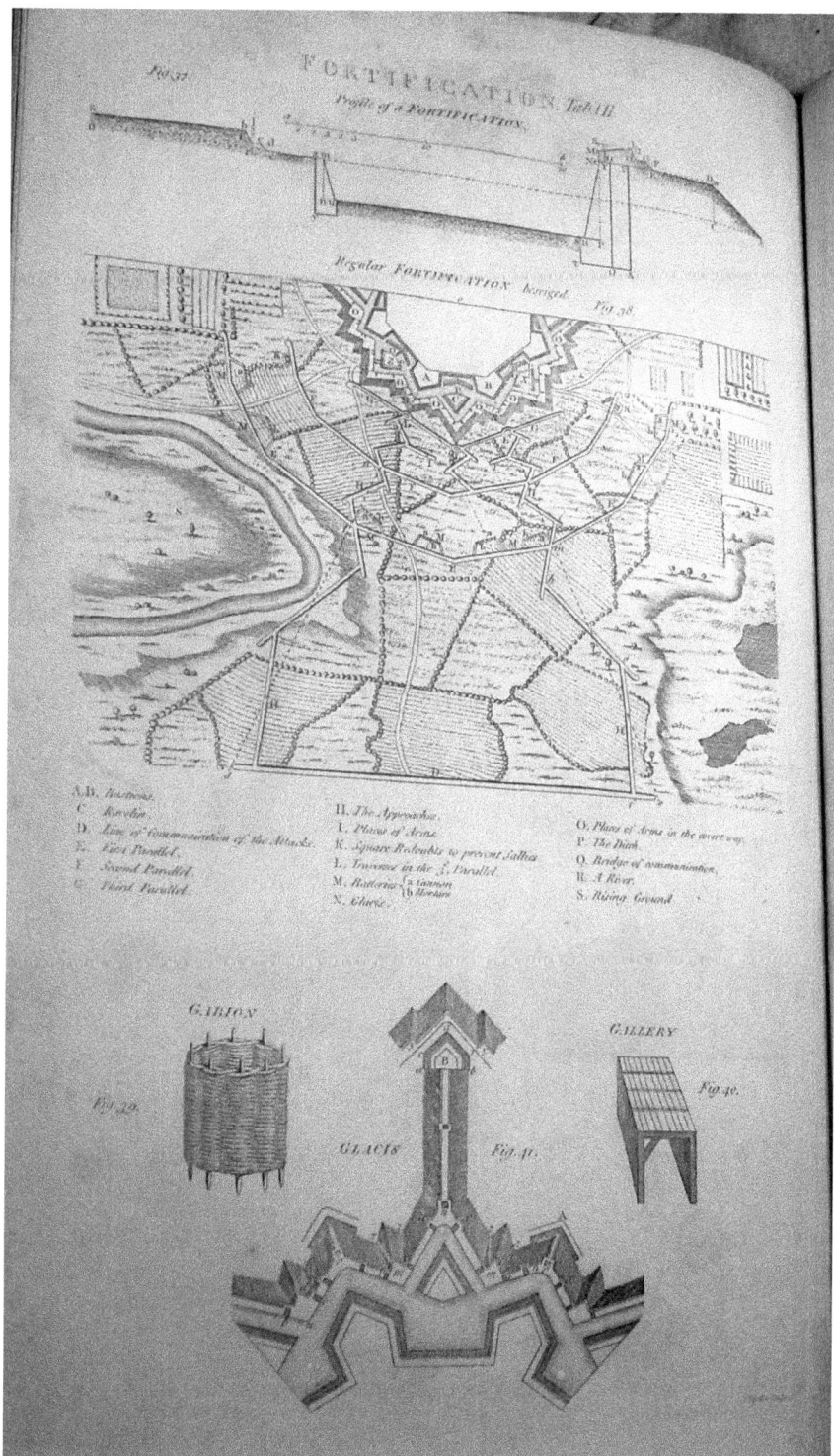

FORTIFICATION. *Tab.III.*

Fig.37.

Profile of a FORTIFICATION.

Regular FORTIFICATION besieged. *Fig.38.*

A,B. *Bastions.*
C. *Ravelin.*
D. *Line of Communication of the Attacks.*
E. *First Parallel.*
F. *Second Parallel.*
G. *Third Parallel.*

H. *The Approaches.*
I. *Places of Arms.*
K. *Square Redoubts to prevent Sallies.*
L. *Traverse in the 3. Parallel.*
M. *Batteries {a cannon {b Mortars.*
N. *Choir.*

O. *Places of Arms in the covert way.*
P. *The Ditch.*
Q. *Bridge of communication.*
R. *A River.*
S. *Rising Ground.*

GABION

GALLERY

Fig.39.

Fig.40.

GLACIS *Fig.41.*

FORTIFICATION *Tab. VIII*

CYCLOPÆDIA

www.ingramcontent.com/pod-product-compliance
Lightning Source LLC
Chambersburg PA
CBHW081630040426
42449CB00014B/3253